GRABBING A SLICE OF "MINNESOTA NICE"

LUCAS LAMONT

GRABBING A SLICE

OF "MINNESOTA NICE"

4 Horsemen
Publications, Inc.

Accomplishing
Innovation Press

Published By: Accomplishing Innovation Press an imprint of 4 Horsemen Publications, Inc.

Accomplishing Innovation Press
℅ 4 Horsemen Publications, Inc.
PO Box 419
Sylva, NC 28779
4horsemenpublications.com
info@4horsemenpublications.com

Cover & Typesetting by Autumn Skye
Edited by Jen Paquette

Library of Congress Control Number: 2024938334

Paperback ISBN-13: 979-8-8232-0429-3
Hardcover ISBN-13: 979-8-8232-0430-9
Audiobook ISBN-13: 979-8-8232-0545-0
Ebook ISBN-13: 979-8-8232-0428-6

"Uffda!"

-*Ole*

"Ya, I read it. It's different."

-*Sven*

"It's not Garrison Keillor. That's for sure."

-*Lena*

TABLE OF CONTENTS

FOREWORD AND DEDICATIONS:

I grew up in a southern Minnesota town nowhere near walking distance to the wonder that is the Twin Cities Area. It took me several years after high school graduation to appreciate the overall serenity of the quiet rural existence, the closeness of its citizens, and the quirks which came from living in the great state.

This memoir is a love letter to the experience I had growing up, the people I grew up with, and the memories I will cherish forever. You may have to squint to see it, but I truly do love the North Star State. My goal is to not only educate you about some of the more noteworthy places I have been to, but also share some insights about the lives and cultures of those who have influenced my life today.

DISCLAIMER:
A MUST READ

1. This first and foremost is to be enjoyed as satirical entertainment. Although there is plenty of accurate information regarding histories, locations, residencies, and other fun facts, any opinions or viewpoints are 100% personal and do not reflect accuracy or truth of any specific person, identifiable groups and locations, or the State of Minnesota itself.

2. Information here is full of personal bias to a common theme of life experiences in a rural area. There is no assumption that the opinions presented fully apply, only apply, or even apply at all to anyone based on rural/urban living.

3. This is a short, fun, light-hearted read! This is NOT my life's story or the official history of everything that happened in the great State of Minnesota. Found something missing I should have included in here? Thanks for noticing.

4. I do not support harassment in the form of communication or actions out of hate including threats, physical violence, prejudice, close-mindedness, or ridicule in any way—especially from reading the content presented here. Be kind or, at the very least, passive aggressive. (A Minnesotan would be!)

5. I *do* support high-fives, heart symbols, smiles, peeing a little bit from laughing too hard, and donations to any of your favorite Minnesota organizations. (Please do not donate body parts, body organs, bodily fluids, disregarded pets, unwanted family members, or past presidential candidates.)

For those who know:
Please help yourself to some coffee and bars.
Go Muskies!

VELKOMMEN!

(That's Norwegian for "welcome" or as
I like to remember it: "Well, come in.")

Welcome to the best State the Union has to offer. We are known first and foremost for having over 10,000 lakes within our borders. But if you're a visitor from "beyond the borders" and didn't come for our lakes, odds are you are here for one of the following: the Mall of America, the Arts District, an exciting Minnesota Wild game, a (hopefully) Superbowl-winning Vikings game, an "I hope they play 'the Wheaties Box years' good" Twins game, snowmobiling, any variation of a family gathering, traffic court, or driving from here to there via I-90 or I-35 (and then coming back once again for traffic court). Whatever brought you here: the citizens of the great state are here to treat you like one of our own.

What is "Minnesota Nice," you ask? It's not simply one word or action. It's a way of life. To describe it in a single sentence or merely one action would be doing a great disservice to anyone and everyone who has ever experienced the intricate phenomenon. Why? For starters, there is such a thing as Minnesota Nice: the idea that we are truly the nicest state in the country. (Put your hand down, Iowa; this isn't an opinion.) And then there's the other side which is *also* called "Minnesota Nice." *This* is the perfected craft in which its citizens express criticism or disappointment in the hopes of avoiding any hurt feelings on the matter. But even both of these definitions, no matter how accurate, don't truly express just how all-encompassing this phenomenon is. And it certainly doesn't address all the nuances.

Outsiders may simply want to define it as passive. To this I say: it is simply not true. It's much more involved and much more layered. Being passive assumes we always find something wrong. Quite frankly, I find it to be the opposite. Minnesotans typically like to hone-in on the one thing that's right. That's where the "nice" comes in. Everyone starts on a clean slate. Everyone gets the benefit of the doubt. And everyone is judged *after* the first impression. (It's *after* the first impression because we want you to leave so the "judging" part can commence.)

The fact is, Minnesota has a code: You better know what to say and how to act because we won't tell if you if you're doing it right, but we'll definitely get someone *else* to tell you that you're doing it wrong.

Don't worry; I know it's a lot of pressure to deal with. However, if you want people who are straight forward, openly opinionated, and will want to dictate your every move... I suggest going to a different state like Maryland or Texas. Just know you won't be as happy there. Why? Simple. They don't have as many lakes, and their NFL Teams have already won the Superbowl. It's not as exciting going to a Baltimore Ravens or Dallas Cowboys game knowing they could win the title *again.* Nothing compares to watching a Minnesota Vikings game from the comfort of my living room, knowing my home state team is getting paid the same whether they win or lose.

No, no, my friend. You made the right decision coming to Minnesota. This is truly the place you want to be. My gift is to be the Minnesotan who shares my experience. As a resident for over twenty years, I do consider myself well-versed in several Minnesota quintessential topics including art, culture, famous people, food, history, and religion.

Should anyone tell you that my information is inaccurate to your face... I'd say there's a 25% chance their claim is true. However, should you read a 1-star book review under the name "anonimous" (yes, spelled incorrectly) who claims they know Minnesota better than I do—*that* individual is a true Minnesotan, and they indeed have called me out on my deceitful ways.

But the fact is, you aren't here to read my opinions on who to believe. You are here to find out how on earth a small-town Minnesota body gets the inspiration to write a reflective narrative on his upbringing when he only has so much time left on this planet. Did that unmistakable accent just captivate and hypnotize me that much? Did those little quirks just seduce and spellbind me to the point I had to tell the world? To that I say: Absolutely!

If you're a reader who recaptures childhood in this experience like I did, I am very grateful. However, if you are an outsider looking in, you may be lost on several of these intricacies. So, to help you out, each designated topic will be written with both residents and visitors in mind. Hopefully, you will be able to identify with at least one of the couples in the scenarios, so you can feel less awkward that you paid full price for this pitiful thing.

But... before we begin...

BOOK BREAK!

And now… a poem dedicated to the mosquitos:

Literally and Figurately:
You suck!

SWEAR WORDS

...

W hy start with swear words? Because whenever someone wants to learn a foreign language ("Minnesotan" included), everyone wants to know the curse words first. It's just human nature.

Despite "Minnesota Nice" being a real way of life for so many of my brothers and sisters, I do have to confess a brave and startling truth: Minnesotans do swear just like any other state. Well—almost. There are some minor changes. For example, instead of outright saying "Hell," I grew up in a little conservative town that preferred being more creative in their choice words... like saying "H-E-Double-hockey-sticks." I mean, gosh, I was raised in a home where saying the name "Jesus" outside the House of God in the casual context meant road construction in the spring recommenced or the price of corn dropped ten cents. If I said it for any other reason, I was shamefully committing blasphemy.

On the other hand, I will mention there is an exception to the standard courteous rules of swearing. Anytime you are trying to mechanically fix whatever your wife, child, or nephew did to royally mess up the boat, car, or lawnmower, you are gifted free reign to whatever words you would like to use. See? We aren't prudes.

So, without further ado, I present to you our first couple, "Hank & Alice Anderson," as they demonstrate how to correctly give Lip Service. If you're wondering which swear words Minnesotans use in general context and what they mean... please read below...

Hank & Alice Anderson
Albert Lea, Minnesota

Hank is a 55-year-old male who spends Monday-Friday checking the seals on every can of *Ocean Spray* cranberry juice and every weekend staying at least one hundred feet away from the house—usually in the garage but preferably in the local bar. His plaid shirts begged for death about eight years ago, but alas, he still wears them as if the original color was robin's egg blue instead of navy. They're tight in the cuffs, and in the stomach but very loose in the neckline for some reason. Because he spends so much time outdoors, he has a permanent discoloration around his neck from years of tanning without any sunblock and a cranium that his wife swears has molded to the shape of his favorite hat, which his dad bought at a truck stop in 1981.

Alice is a 52-year-old female whose hair color is less than two weeks old. She's a sweet gal who collects loose change in a cigar box so old it doesn't carry the surgeon general's warning label. She regularly goes away to visit the casino on

Sundays after church even though she's telling Hank she's visiting her parents in Iowa. Don't worry; she's not a gambling addict. She alternates weeks on the church offering plate, and Hank doesn't know the wiser. On the first and third weekend, God gets a $50 bill. On the second and fourth, Diamond Jo's Casino gets to keep their lights on another day. If there's a fifth weekend that falls in the month, Alice reflects on how she did on slots the previous weekend. Typically, she'll split her money down the middle: $25 will go back to Diamond Jo, and $25 will be sacrificed in the name of Jesus.

Both lovely residents frequently find themselves in scenarios that invoke the "trucker mouth" or "swearin' like a sailor" bit. No matter what the cause is for such words to be uttered, it will always be done "Minnesotan."

"Gosh"

A word uttered for being excited or overwhelmed.

> Hank: "Oh, gosh! Alice, did you see what the neighbor boy did with PVC Pipe and two golf balls?"
>
> Alice: "A trip to the casino or a new shirt for work? Tough Call. A trip to the casino *and* a new shirt for work? Oh, gosh, I just couldn't!"

An appropriate alternative when not specifically addressing or respectfully referencing his holiness.

> Alice: "Gosh, I wish my son would write church sermons instead of erotic novels."
>
> Hank: "Gosh... that new Ford model would go great in the driveway."

"Darn"

A word uttered for being disappointed.

> Hank: "The bar ran out of Miller Lite again. Darn it. Had to drink Busch."

> Alice: "I would love to watch the football game with you, Hank, but it's Sunday, and you know my parents are expecting me. Darn. Next time!"

An appropriate alternative when not specifically addressing condemnation or respectfully reading religious texts.

> Alice: "That darn cat got into the cookies again! Oh well, Hank won't know the difference."

> Hank: "Alice! What happened to my shirt I've been wearing the past two days? It's in the wash? Darn it all to heck! I was just getting ready to mow the lawn! What am I supposed to wear now?!"

"Gosh-Darn it"

The combo indicating a realization that led to self-disappointment.

> Alice: "I forgot the casserole dish at my parents! Oh, Gosh-Darn it! Guess I'll have to go down next weekend to get it."

> Hank: Hank doesn't say "Gosh-darn it."

"*Jeez*"

A word used to express disbelief.

> Hank: "Aw, Jeez! I knew they said Hwy 169 was bad at 5 p.m., but I didn't know it was *this* bad! Wish I had a beer on me."

> Alice: "$60 for a color and the roots are already coming up? Jeez!"

A reluctantly acceptable alternative when not specifically addressing or respectfully referencing God's only son.

> Hank: "Alice! Did you see the brand-new Chevy Joe just bought? I bet he's going to park that in the driveway every single day just to show it off too. Jeez, when is it my turn?"

> Alice: "If I had a nickel each time Mary walked by the front of the house when I'm watering the yard to tell me I got a few more dandelions to take care of… Jeez, give me strength!"

"Heck"

An appropriate alternative when not specifically addressing or respectfully referencing the fiery underworld.

> Alice: "Go to heck, Hank!" **(Most occasions)**

> Hank: "Heck or high water, whatever you're thinkin', Alice, it's not gonna happen." **(Most occasions)**

A word uttered for being aggravated.

> Alice: "What the heck, Hank?" **(All occasions)**

> Hank: "What the heck you do that for, Alice?!" **(All occasions)**

"Crap"

A word uttered for being frustrated.

> Hank: "Hwy 494 is closed again. Crap!"

Alice: "Oh, I sat next to Judy at the bar again, and she smokes like a chimney. Now Hank is gonna smell it. Crap!"

A questionable alternative for referring to fecal matter.

Alice: "I just washed my car, and now I got all this bird crap all over it!"

Hank: "It doesn't rain for a month, but then I get new boots and it's monsoon season. Now I gotta walk through all that crap just to get to the house."

"Bitch"

The term given to a man's ex-wife.

Hank: "I don't know what's going on this weekend yet. Better ask the 'Bitch' first."

Alice: "I have to wait, Beatrice. Hank doesn't know what's going on with the kids this weekend yet. He has to ask the 'Bitch' first."

A term also given to a woman's best friend when she's not in earshot.

Alice: "I love Beatrice, but last night at the bar, she acted like a total bitch! I still can't wait to be her maid-of-honor tomorrow though!"

Hank: "For the last time, Alice: I don't mind you having Sheila over here. Just let me know in advance so I go in the basement and watch a game so I don't have to hear her bitch!"

"Ass"

The only acceptable curse word on this list.

<u>Alice</u>: "Hank! Wear tighter pants or use a belt! No one wants to see your ass hangin' out!"

<u>Hank</u>: "Lauren is on vacation. He's out for two weeks and now I'm in charge of the forklift. Thanks, Lauren. You ass."

"Whatever"

The word used continuously throughout the 1990s that finally told Minnesota it was okay to be passive aggressive. Don't know what the essence of the word means? Then you weren't an annoying kid, angsty teenager, or jaded parent in that decade. Here's your hint: When directly told to or said in response to another person's comment or viewpoint, it is an invitation to stop the current conversation complete with the "F" word. Don't believe me? Let's share a very 1990s viewpoint and give it a very 1990s response...

> <u>Hank</u>: "I'm telling you, O.J. is innocent! That man loved his wife like all men should love their wives."

> <u>Alice</u>: "Whatever, Hank." (Extra points for the "stop" hand gesture, eye roll, and head turn.)

"The F-Word"

We know there are less damaging ways to say it. But we don't like those either.

> <u>Hank</u>: "I don't know what the 'F' you were thinking? You know better than to use farm diesel in a regular truck!"

> <u>Alice</u>: "I said I let her *borrow* it! If Melanie thinks she's keeping my Tupperware, she's out of her 'F-ing' mind!"

"Green Bay Packers"

If you fancy this team, please read the sermon "Sinners in The Hands of an Angry God" by Jonathan Edwards. We devoted Vikings fans will drink a beer (or four) while we wait. Don't worry; in the end, we'll still accept you... Minnesota "nicely."

Cue the ominous music

<No example sentence provided. If you need one, I refer you to both examples for the word "Heck.">

So? What do you think? Are you a true Minnesotan yet? Of course, you're not! If anything, I'm sure you have more questions than answers after reading that first section. The most obvious being: Why does Hank still let Alice use the "going to her parents" cover-up story for the casino trips considering her parents have been dead for two years? Unfortunately, I can't answer everything. But one thing I can say for sure is: Hank isn't going to feel guilty when he pulls into the driveway in that brand new Ford truck next week!

BOOK BREAK!

And now... a comment to the road construction from April - September:

Someone tell Elon Musk to invest in hover craft!

FOOD

Nothing is more recognizable in a culture than food. By the age of ten, most individuals can look at a classic dish and guess its origins:

1. Lo Mein—China

2. Lasagna—Italy

3. Frankfurter—Germany

4. Tortillas—Mexico

5. Curry—India

6. Soylent Green—United States

Once in your hands, food instantly grabs three out of the five senses and commands them to pay attention. As for the remaining two senses (sound and taste), it is of course situational. For example, if you are "hearing" your food, we hope the sound of it is more along the lines of "Snap, Crackle, and Pop" from your bowl of Rice Krispies and not the final gasps of Bambi's mom. To be fair, when it comes to "taste," we'd rather you be judging the flavor of Bambi's mom versus the flavor of Hansel and Gretel. In the end, though, we'll be "Minnesota Nice" to both parties. After all, hunters and cannibals are people, too.

As for myself, I can say I have tried most of the iconic foods the state offers. That may not be noteworthy on the surface, but the fact is, you don't realize just how unique some of the options are until you enter (or leave) the state for the first time. One of the best examples I can give you is the social understanding of the word "sushi." In the other 49 states, it is a proud Japanese tradition where rice and seaweed are accompanied by raw fish and perhaps a vegetable or two. But in Minnesota, when I'm at the annual summer family reunion in Putman Park under the picnic shelter in 90-degree heat, and I ask if someone brought "sushi," I am gestured to a picnic table full of colorful Tupperware showing me combinations Japan probably hasn't even heard of.

First, there is the quintessential pickle roll-up: a dill pickle wrapped in deli meat (preferably ham) with a layer of cream cheese. Once sliced, the appearance gives off a shiny jade color which tells a Minnesotan the party has arrived... or tells an unsuspecting Japanese traditionalist something has gone wrong with the tuna.

Second, another Minnesota classic is the Snicker Salad. "Salad" is very loosely used here as the only redeeming healthy quality in the concoction is freshly chopped Granny Smith apples. Otherwise, instant French vanilla pudding and whipped cream are folded together with... you guessed it... a chopped-up Snickers bar. The minute you set this cold salad out on a hot day, your Minnesota family will flock to it. I, however, had the unique experience of setting this potluck dish out at a party in Seattle, Washington, where most guests collectively decided I was trying to poison them with what they couldn't visibly see in the creamy opaque goop. Sorry, Seattle. I'm just being my Minnesota self. The punchline to the Seattle gathering? They had *real*, authentic sushi there, too.

Charlie Thompson & Jane Berg (featuring Jane's mother)
Minneapolis, Minnesota

Jane's 30th birthday is upon her. The milestone has her continuously remembering her family's heritage and all the comforts of living on the farm. Like other women who don't take anti-depressants, her drug of choice is anything Weight Watchers wouldn't approve of. So, for the next few pages, the cookbook from her local church and *Kraft Magazine* will be her besties.

Charlie is considerably older than Jane but also considerably less Minnesotan than her. They met a year ago after his job at Target Corp. transferred him from Chicago to Minneapolis. Now they live together unmarried and unashamed. Being a fellow man from the Midwest, Charlie didn't think Minnesota would be that different. To his credit, he did find a *few* things that were the same. He recalls seeing corn in Chicago in its natural form once… and it was even on display for its intended use: eating! Who knew?! But Charlie couldn't fathom the traditions Jane would subject him to nor how much she'd live and die by them!

Unannounced, Jane's mother has come into town to help celebrate/comfort Jane on her birthday. She's a woman of strength who has survived four children, five careers, and eight two-term presidents. Yes, her husband could have come along for the weekend… but at the last minute, Jane's mother didn't invite him.

"Corn"

Corn and Minnesota are one-and-the-same. There's a good reason why Rochester, Minnesota, has erected a water tower in honor of it. When I figure out precisely what that good reason was, I'll let you know.

Charlie: *In Bubba's voice from *Forrest Gump** "Corn-on-the-cob, grilled corn, fried corn, scalloped corn, creamed corn, corn chowder, corn bread, corn dogs, corn nuts, and corn-... wait? I don't remember eating corn?!"

Jane: "Well, don't you worry. We're having something different tonight! Corn salsa with corn tortilla chips!"

Then there was that one incident...

Jane's mother: *Stares at Charlie in disbelief* "Charlie, you idiot! We don't eat *that* kind of corn! No, we don't. Because it's a decoration. That's why it's so colorful! You just put it in an arrangement on the table. You... fine! Boil it. Have fun."

"Hot dish"

I've heard other states call this a "casserole." The biggest difference? If you come across a Minnesota hot dish, it means there were no rules or regulations for what went in it. Why do you think you find it at church gatherings so much? May God protect you during and after its consumption.

> Jane: "I didn't have time to make something fancy, so I just whipped up a hot dish."
>
> Jane's mother: "You followed *my* recipe and not Aunt Jennifer's in the church cookbook, right?"
>
> Charlie: "You know, when I was growing up, a 'hot dish' was when you could get HBO to come through on the satellite feed after midnight without paying for it."

"Tater Tot Hot Dish"

The hot dish to top all other hot dishes: crispy golden tater tots and overcooked hamburger meat, all smothered in a can of mushroom soup. There's a special place in Hell for those who add vegetables to it.

Jane: "I haven't had this in years!"

Jane's mother: "When you were a kid, I'd make this once a week. It was one of the only meals you'd eat."

Charlie: "Only in Minnesota will a state sanction Tater Tot Hot Dish as a regular menu item in the places we educate our youth."

"Jucy Lucy" or "Juicy Lucy"

A cheese-stuffed hamburger. Like a good Minnesotan, I'll let someone else tell you which bar in Minneapolis invented it.

Charlie: "It's a piece of cheese in the middle of a hamburger. Why is it such a big deal which bar invented it?"

Jane: "You did not just say that."

Jane's mother: "Sweetheart, are you sure you aren't considering other suitors? Does he have to be 'the one'? Maybe he has a brother? Or preferably a very distant cousin?"

"Sloppy Joes"

I couldn't really tell you who "Joe" was or why he was "Sloppy," but other states call these sandwiches "Bar-B-Ques," "Loose Meat sandwiches," or "Slush Burgers." Wisconsin had a seizure and calls them "Hot Tamales," and Iowa just being Iowa calls them "Maid-Rites." (In Iowa's defense, they do cite this as a different concoction all together. But in *our* defense, it's still Iowa saying it.) Uncultured people go the commercial route and call them "Manwiches" after the goop in the can they expect you to add to your 73/27 hamburger meat. (Fine, use the stuff in the can. Just don't tell anyone.)

> Jane: "Mom, there's still something missing in the sauce!"
>
> Jane's mother: "Add ketchup and mustard."
>
> Jane: "I already did. That's not it."
>
> Charlie: "You put ketchup and mustard in the Sloppy Joe sauce?!"
>
> Jane's mother: "Get out of the kitchen, Charlie."

"Margarine"

Yes, it's cheaper; yes, it's a bait and switch, but we'll still refer to it as "butter." We're partial to Country Crock. Why? Because after Hormel bought the license to use it in their own products, we adopted it as a Minnesota-allied food ever since.

> Jane's mother: "Charlie, be a dear and grab the butter from the fridge."

Charlie: ***Searches frantically*** "I don't see 'butter.' All I see is 'margarine.'"

Jane's mother: "That's what I said!"

Charlie: ***Scratches his head*** "But this says 'margarine.'"

Jane: "It's butter."

Charlie: "But—"

Jane: "It's butter."

Charlie: "How?"

Jane's mother: "It's better."

Charlie: "I think the beer is calling me."

"Cheese"

Wisconsin's only respectable contribution.

Jane's mother: "I found this great recipe under 'light healthy snacks'... It contains cheddar cheese, parmesan cheese, cream cheese, heavy cream, bacon, garlic salt, and whole milk. Serve with carrot sticks."

Jane: "I saw that recipe in *Kraft Magazine*! They say you can substitute the cream cheese for low fat yogurt and save 40 calories per serving!"

Charlie: "But then you just sit there and eat double the amount, which completely erases the whole point of using low fat yogurt in the first place. Am I right?"

Jane's mother: "Jane, can you hand me the corkscrew."

Jane: "Sure. But this bottle of Sutter Home wine is a screw cap."

Jane's mother: "I know that, sweetheart." ***Eyes Charlie***

"Nuts"

The ultimate beer snack; Planters, the once-Pennsylvanian company, sold to Minnesota's own Hormel in February 2021. Taste those nuts, Minnesota. Taste all those nuts!

Charlie: "I remember the days when you'd go to a bar, get served a cold beer with a basket of nuts, and you'd just throw all the shells on the floor."

Jane: "The Ground Round did that when I was a kid!"

Jane's mother: "Those poor waitresses… constantly sweeping and vacuuming up peanut shells every day. They never would have made a man do that."

Charlie: "Men don't look good vacuuming."

Jane's mother: "That's because the task is so simple. The easier the task is, the easier it is for a man to mess it up. And they *always* mess it up."

Charlie: "You know, Jane, I hear it's supposed to snow on Sunday. Might have to cut the trip short to Saturday so you don't get stuck here."

Jane's mother: "Oh, I have no plans to leave before Sunday. So, my suggestion to you is: pray for rain."

Jane: "Charlie? Where are you going?"

Charlie: "To get more beer in case we get snowed in."

Odds are your grandmother didn't know how to make a dessert without them.

Jane: "Yeah… sorry, mom. Charlie doesn't like walnuts in his desserts, so we're gonna to have to skip them this time."

Jane's mother: "What do you mean you don't like nuts, Charlie? There are nuts in everything! There are nuts in the brownies, nuts in the cake, nuts in the cookies, nuts in the pudding, nuts in the ice cream, and nuts in the banana bread! The only place you won't find nuts is in Jane's father. And those took *years* to get rid of!"

"Salted Nut Roll"

A crown jewel of candy bars we are proud to say comes from our state. Good job, Pearson.

> <u>Jane's mother</u>: "A Snickers is good, an Almond Joy is better, but nothing beats a Pearson's Salted Nut Roll."

> <u>Charlie</u>: "I like a Tootsie Roll, myself."

> <u>Jane's mother</u>: "That's acceptable."

> <u>Charlie</u>: "Thank God."

"Rocky Mountain Oysters"

Bull testicles which are eaten so men don't have to be envious of them anymore. Despite the decision to eat this otherwise lewd body part, the name stays classy so people will think they're eating a *delicacy* versus something they might want to eat *delicately*.

Based on reviews, the preference is deep fried.

> Charlie: "Men call it 'Victory.'"

> Jane's mother: "Women call it 'Justice.'"

"Pickled" (foods)

We challenge you tell us it can't be pickled: fish, eggs, vegetables, turkey, pork, your childhood dog, your grandmother's dog, your grandmother, and of course, Cher.

> Jane's mother: "If I could turn back time, I wouldn't need to be pickled."

> Charlie: "If I could turn time *forward*, it would be quieter in this house."

> Jane's mother: "I'm still not leaving until Sunday."

"Spam"

The common theme in several Minnesota-based foods is the natural (or unnatural) wonder of preservation. Easily traced back to many Nordic traditions and then amplified by the harsh realities of two World Wars and the Great Depression, across the entire state is the blood-bound philosophy to never let anything go to waste. This can easily be summed up in the most iconic preserved food ever created in the entire world: The Hormel Company's very own Spam. In short, its contents are based on minced pork shoulder pressed into a mold and salted beyond belief. Several recommendations include Spam and Eggs, Spam Burgers, Spam Hot Dish, Spam Loaf (don't ask), and finally, Spam in the trash can.

Jane's mother: "Don't worry. If you regret throwing an unopened can of Spam away, you can dig it out of the landfill six months later. It will still be good."

Charlie: "I don't understand. What is it exactly?"

Jane's mother: "It's Spam."

Charlie: "But what is it?"

Jane & Jane's mother: *In unison* "It's Specially Processed American Meat!"

Charlie: "Whiskey! I'm switching to whiskey!"

"Lutefisk"

A Nordic tradition typically consisting of codfish cured in lye to turn it into a preserved gelatinous clump of sadness beloved by older generations and shunned by the younger.

Jane's mother: "Charlie, have you ever had lutefisk?"

Charlie: "No."

Jane's mother: "Would you like to try some lutefisk?"

Charlie: "No."

"Walleye"

A freshwater yellow pike or pickerel; the steak of the lake; the fish in that long-ass story grandpa tells every time you visit as if it's the first time you've heard it.

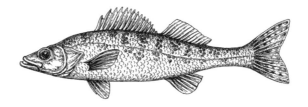

Jane's mother: "Jane, if your father was here, he'd say: 'This lake is nothing like when I was kid. Back in my day, you'd pull out 20 Walleye in twenty minutes.'"

Charlie: "You over-fished it, developed all the land around it, and then dumped farm chemical into it. Thanks, Boomer."

"Wild Rice"

The food Native Americans grow and cultivate and Nordic Immigrants proudly take credit for as part of their heritage.

Jane's mother: "Worth its weight in gold—no really—have you seen the prices for this stuff? We've never appreciated Uncle Ben's Wild Rice more than now."

"Venison"

A traditionally heavily seasoned lean meat from "game" animals including deer, elk, antelope, and hares. If you don't judge us, we'll tell you what it is before you try it. If you *do* judge us, we'll have you try it *before* we tell you.

Charlie: "When's dinner? I'm hungry!"

Jane: "Here, Charlie. My mom brought some of that jerky you like."

Charlie: "Finally, a food from your mother I don't have to be afraid of." ***Moments later*** "By the way, what is this stuff? I've never found any supermarket that has anything that tastes like this."

Jane's mother: "Last summer I had that darn pesky deer going after my garden. Jane's father took care of it."

Charlie: "What does that have to do with beef jerky?"

Jane: "Babe, this was never beef jerky. It was venison jerky."

Charlie: ***Swallows hard*** "I've been eating Bambi meat?"

"Vegetarian/Vegan"

Why would you do that?

Charlie: "You wanna tell me how that happened?"

Jane's mother: "Well, Jane was fine with raising a calf since birth. But when we told her the steak she was eating was the calf she used to bottle-feed... I don't know?! I guess *that's* when she said she was going 'Vegetarian.'"

Charlie: "No future wife of mine is going to be a vegetarian! Now grab that rifle. We're going hunting."

"Bars"

The most common dessert brought to a gathering by a middle-aged woman carrying the stressful burden of a full-time job, kids, a husband, and years of regret.

Essentially, you are staring at one large cookie baked in a pan. That's if you can actually *see* the cookie underneath the toppings of cereal, nuts, frosting, cream cheese, marshmallows, chocolate, whipped cream, and whatever else was getting ready to expire. Who says dessert can't be considered a meal?

Charlie: "What is this?"

Jane: "It's dessert."

Charlie: "But what is it?"

Jane: "It's a bar."

Charlie: "But what *is* it?"

Jane's mother: "It's a 'Scotcheroo.'"

Charlie: "You're right, Jane. It's dessert."

"Jell-O Salad"

The salad to end all other salads. Preferably green. At some point, Minnesotans decided any food folded into whipped cream was a "salad." For years, schools silently praised the state for saying ketchup (or "Catsup") was a vegetable in order to keep costs down. So, I'm going to go out on a limb and say some Minnesotans consider "Jell-O" a fruit.

<u>Jane's mother</u>: "Oh, Jeez! Quit rolling your eyes! Throw some pear chunks or mandarin oranges in it, for God's sake! If you don't stop your whining, I'll throw nuts in it!"

"Potluck"

Where you contribute a food item toward a meal gathering (even if we said you didn't need to bring anything). *This is to be brought to the function already prepped or premade.* And whatever you bring, it better be worthy of the other things on the spread.

Charlie: "What's Aunt Jennifer mad about from last summer?"

Jane's mother: "The family reunion last year—the main meal was designed as a potluck. Jane said you two were going to bring potato salad."

Charlie: "We did!"

Jane's mother: "You did... but you brought a pre-packaged salad from the store."

Charlie: "What's wrong with that?"

Jane's mother: "Aunt Jennifer was convinced you should have gone through the church cookbook and picked out her recipe and made it, or if you wanted it to taste good, *my* recipe."

Jane: "I feel bad, Mom! I really do. We were just so busy with work…"

Jane's mother: "I know, sweetheart. You're just not ready to handle the responsibility of 'The Potato Salad' yet. One day you will."

Jane: *sobs uncontrollably*

"Starbucks"

What you drinkin' that expensive stuff for?

Charlie: "I got the ritual Saturday morning Starbucks. I even got you one!"

Jane's mother: *Points to Charlie's cup* "What's that? I've never seen one that big!"

Charlie: "Oh! Did you know there's an extra-large size you can order that they don't advertise?"

Jane's mother: "And how much did that set you back?"

Charlie: *Points to his own cup* "This alone was $10."

Jane's mother: "For that price, I could have brewed you about five gallons here at home."

Charlie: "But I like coffee you can't actually see through. Plus, I want somethin' that has taste."

Jane's mother: "You know what you can't taste, Charlie?"

Charlie: "Your home-brewed coffee?" *Smiles*

Jane's mother: "Arsenic." *Smiles back*

"IPA Beer"

Bars in small towns with populations less than 3,000 found themselves scratching their head when this trend swept through. Mainly, it was because they didn't know what "IPA" stood for, and they didn't want to ask.

Charlie: "If I can't see through it, don't know what it is, and have to guess what the letters mean, I don't trust it. Don't you have Coors, Bud, or Busch?"

I hope that with the segment on food, you've really enriched yourself in some Minnesota culture. Charlie himself has really grown to understand and appreciate the rich taste that only Minnesotan sustenance can provide. And for those of you who have any concerns, I promise you, Jane's mother was returned home in a condition which did not require her body to go into a casket or mason jar. Charlie, however, needed a day off from work, a lot of water, and a few Tylenol.

BOOK BREAK!

And now... an explanation on voting Walter Mondale and Jesse Ventura into public office:

We were high on the methane fumes from the dairy farms.

NEW-COMER HOSPITALITY

Y ou sure are lucky to be here in the great state of Minnesota if you are new from beyond the border. I can only imagine the stories local historical societies must have told children after the Great Depression about how innocent, unsuspecting Minnesotans traveled to the other surrounding states and died from dehydration or hunger. From then on, we made sure that no one would ever experience the same when coming to our glorious state. And believe it or not, no matter where you're from, we'll give you the same hospitality. That's right, Iowa, North Dakota, South Dakota, Nebraska, and that other state we shall not name. We'll treat you right. But just know there are some rules and expectations to receiving this hospitality. No one is ever going to tell you this in person, so consider this mercy onto you.

Me? I consider myself spoiled. When I visit a native Minnesotan's home, I already know two things: #1 I don't have to eat in advance because I will be fed a four course meal if I time it right, and #2 I need to pack my toothbrush and a clean pair of underwear in case the visit turns into an overnighter. Living outside the state now has been difficult to adjust to. Visiting friends and family who aren't familiar with Minnesota customs also lets me know two things: #1 I'll be sent a bill for those five potato chips I ate—even if I was offered them in the first place—and #2 My host already knows I'm leaving in an hour—even if I don't.

Pat & Debra Nelson (featuring Maria Flores)
Marshall, Minnesota

I sense you getting frustrated that you are not fully acclimated yet. I know what you're thinking: it's unfair that all my scenarios are with Minnesota natives who are completely comfortable with the language and culture. But what about when you do have someone who is a stranger to the wonderful state? I hear your concerns and will now provide you with scenarios which will fully address how Minnesotans talk to the outsiders and interlopers. I present you with the following...

Pat is that quintessential Minnesotan small business owner who owns a General Store. He inherited the business from *his* father who inherited the business from *his* father who won the business in a poker tournament from a man whose father politely asked the Sioux Indians to now consider the land as private property. Like many small business owners, Pat has spent his entire adult life fighting off big government and even bigger corporations to keep him from going under. But he's a survivor and will continue to be all the way to his 200th birthday.

Debra is Pat's wife. She appears white due to her Swedish background, but she is actually part Sioux herself. Depending on the season, her tone favors one ethnicity over the other.

When she stays indoors during the winter, she skews very Swedish. And when she tans during the summer, all her neighbors call her "Sioux-per Swedish." Debra knows a lot about her Native American heritage and even a few words of her ancestral language. However, she has yet to tell her husband Pat that the word "wife" in Native American means "The *real* owner of the General Store." Everyone *else* knows it, of course. She manages that place with an iron fist!

Maria just moved to town with her family and was looking for part time work while her husband works full-time in the fields and their children are at school. Debra was more than happy to welcome Maria to town as well as their place of business but has clearly sensed the young lady is out of her comfort zone. To help acclimate her, Debra has invited Maria over to her home as a guest. It is through the eyes of Maria that you will understand what it is like to be a guest to a Minnesota-grown family.

"Water"

First and foremost, we will always offer you a glass of water. Don't ever expect it to be bottled water unless something is wrong with the plumbing or water system.

Whether it's bottled or tap water, there's an 80% chance you are getting it room temperature and/or straight from the faucet. Please don't ask for ice. Yes, we have it, but it's inconvenient to the process. Just count your lucky stars if ice is offered to you.

> Debra: "Please have a seat in the kitchen, Maria." *Sits down to join her guest* "Where are my manners? Would you like a glass of water?"
>
> Maria: "Yes, please. Thank you."
>
> Debra: "Of course." *Effortlessly floats off the chair, barely making a noise. Joyfully hums to

herself while thinking life can't get better than this. Pulls out thick plastic cup and fills it from the sink with tap water. Sets down the glass gently in front of Maria and softly lands herself back in her chair next to Maria.*

Maria: *Takes a sip of the scalding hot tap water which has baked in the sun from July's heat wave* "May I trouble you for some ice?"

Debra: "Sure." *Chair screeches back from the table in slow motion as Debra hoists her old body back up. Every bone creaks and every muscle aches as she remembers the torture she suffered from yesterday's BOGO sale at the General Store. Her hand trembles as she struggles to steady the glass back to the freezer and begrudgingly spares two cubes from the sacred chamber. As one cube falls into the near-boiling glass of water, she dies a little inside. As the second cube falls in, throwing steam back at her face, she dies a little more. The glass finally is set back in front of Maria, and she places herself, not next to, but directly across from her guest, watching, waiting*

Maria: "Thank you."

Debra: "No problem at all."

Fortunately, your chances of being offered ice in your water goes up 10% starting at a summer outdoor temperature of 90 degrees. For example: 90 degrees = 10% chance, 91 degrees = 20%. However, your chances stop all together once it reaches 96 degrees. Why? Because if the temperature is 96 degrees or above outside, and you ring the doorbell, we're not answering it. The air conditioning can barely keep up as it is, and we're not opening the door.

<u>Maria</u>: ***Knocks on the door*** "Deb, are you home?"

<u>Debra</u>: ***Squints at the outdoor thermostat and gasps*** "No, sorry. We're not."

<u>Maria</u>: "But I hear you! Didn't you just invite me over?"

<u>Debra</u>: "I know, but I just found out we're out of coffee. I hear next week is supposed to be cooler—erm, I mean, I hear next week coffee is on sale. How about we do a raincheck until then?"

<u>Maria</u>: ***Fans herself over the July heat as the sun burns off the top layer of skin*** "I don't need coffee, Deb. It's too hot. We can just chat over a glass of water."

<u>Debra</u>: ***Long silence*** "We're out of water."

<u>Maria</u>: "Is something wrong? I can barely hear you." ***No response*** "Listen, it's really hot out, so I'm just going to open the door and—"

<u>Debra</u>: "NOOOOOOOOOOO!!!!!!!"

"Beer"

Something about this drink has really made its home in the Great State of Minnesota. During the summer, you'll find it as the number one drink on the lake, pulled from many coolers stuffed with ice. During the winter, you'll find it as the number one drink on the lake, pulled from God's bountiful cooler, aptly named: the snowbank.

As far as hospitality goes, there are only two scenarios in Minnesota in which you will be offered a beer...

#1) You are indeed a welcomed guest: a friend, family member, or an extension of either.

> Debra: "Maria, want a beer?"

> Maria: "After working yesterday's BOGO Sale? Absolutely!"

After Maria took her first sip, she and Debra discussed how to stop world hunger and restore peace in the Middle East

#2) The more unfortunate scenario is this: you are a complete stranger who was brought into our home by someone we "trusted" but had no advance warning. Other than the proverbial question which explains how in the heck you fit in the picture, you'll get asked if you want a beer because, in actuality, *we* want a beer. At some point, we hope the alcohol in our system will make your presence less awkward. As for the guest we trusted *not* to put us in this position in the first place? They're on watch.

> Pat: ***Stares awkwardly*** "Who's this?"

Debra: "Pat, this is Maria! Our new employee! Jeez!"

Pat: "Oh! Welcome!" **More awkward silence** "Would you like a beer?"

Debra: **Glances at her watch** "It's 10 a.m. on Sunday!"

Pat: "Are you Catholic?"

Maria: "Yes."

Pat: "Do you want wine, instead?"

"Coffee"

Please bear in mind, this is the one, and ONLY drink you will be offered that if it is not already made, we will make it fresh for you. Well, not so much for you, but because *we* want it fresh.

Debra: "I'm so delighted you came over this morning. I'll make some coffee." **Reaches for the coffee grinder and fresh whole-bean coffee**

Maria: "I'd love a cup. Thank you."

Debra: "I hope you don't mind waiting."

Maria: "Waiting for a fresh brew? Not at all!"

Are you getting offered instant coffee? Just know that you did something wrong. We won't tell you what it is, but you did it. The other alternative, of course, is we're giving you instant because we'd prefer you leave sooner rather than later.

Debra: "I'm so delighted you came over this morning. I'll make some coffee." ***Reaches for the coffee grinder and fresh whole-bean coffee***

Maria: "I'd love a cup. Thank you. By the way, when I was at the store yesterday, I noticed there was a crack in the floor, a hole in the ceiling, and a leak in the bathroom."

Debra: "You don't say!" ***Process immediately slows to a halt. A smooth transition to the container of instant coffee crystals commences***

"Wine"

If the box is already open, yeah, sure, we'll part with a glass. Two if you're special.

Debra: "Maria, I'm in the mood to celebrate. Will you be a dear and fetch the wine from the fridge while I grab the glasses? It's in the fridge. No, it's there. It's the box. There's a sack... just pull on the sack. If you want it to come out, you have to pull harder on the sack. There you go! Now push down on the nipple but be careful! The harder you push, the faster it squirts out. Phew! Made it!"

"Tea"

My recommendation is not to ask nor accept the offering of tea. The tea bags are about 10 years old, and the only reason we have them is because Aunt Edna died last year, and we didn't have the heart to throw them away.

Debra: "Are you a tea drinker, Maria? I can make you a cup. Gosh, I have so many." ***Asks innocently*** "Would you like to take some home?"

Maria: ***Investigates the offer—stares cautiously at the small print, which indicates a hard-to-read date with a four-digit year that starts with a "1" and not a "2"*** "I am, but I have plenty of my own."

Debra: "Do you have enough Green?"

Maria: "Yes."

Debra: "Herbal?"

Maria: "Of course."

Debra: "Oolong, Earl Grey, Jasmine, Ginger, Chamomile?"

Maria: "I don't need—"

Debra: *Pleads desperately* "Take it from me!" *Smiles* "Please."

"A Sandwich"

For food, let's start at the Holy Grail of offerings because it's only gonna get worse from here.

If you are getting offered a sandwich, recognize you are a top tier guest getting the experience of what Minnesota hospitality is all about. But let's bring this offering down to reality, shall we? This isn't going to be some delicatessen sandwich from a bistro in St. Paul. This is going to be a simple offering to accomplish nothing else other than curing hunger pangs. (Nutritional value is not guaranteed.) You will be served two slices of white bread, a generous layer of margarine or butter, and one thin slice of ham.

Debra: "One slice. No, one slice. You get *one*!"

And please, please, please, do not ask for mayonnaise or mustard. We don't want to be put into that awkward position if we don't have it. (Odds are we do, but we need it for the potato salad recipe this weekend.) More importantly, it's another shock to the system and the process. It's not what we prepared for.

Maria: "Do you have any spicy mustard?"

Debra: *Mumbles to herself* "I knew I should have just offered a few crackers. Here I am getting out the bread, getting out the ham, getting out the margarine, getting out the mustard, getting out a knife, a plate, a napkin. She's going to want a drink with it. That's going to take a glass. Now I've just created half a sink's worth of dishes."

"Candy"

Okay, let's be real. We've been sitting in the kitchen having an enjoyable conversation over our fresh brewed cup of coffee, but in the 20 minutes you've been here, you've been indirectly speaking to the candy dish at the center of the table. Yes, you can have one, even two. Heck, we'll even let you break tradition here and let you take it without asking. It's not as if we care. It was last year's Halloween candy anyway.

Debra: ***Picks up the open decorative jar and offers it*** "Would you like one of the soft chews? They're my favorite."

Maria: "Sure! They're my favorite, too!" ***Rubs fingers together in excited anticipation and finally selects a toffee-flavored soft chew***

Debra: ***Watches intently, as if the entire experience was a science experiment on testing the viability of overprocessed sugar***

Maria: ***Enthusiastically pops the sweet into her mouth and attempts to chew it as intended. After the first pass, her jaw instantly freezes like an unplanned pileup in the conveyer belt system of an assembly line. Instead, she tries to validate the claim that the tongue is the strongest muscle in the body as she uses it to pry the sticky object out of her back molar.***

Debra: "They're good, aren't they?!"

Maria: ***Slowly nods, wondering if Debra is either taking medication which alters her sanity or is out of medication designed to keep it in place*** "So good." ***She stresses as she hopes the dental plan covers cracked teeth***

"Cake"

We'll gladly offer you a piece of cake when you come over if we have it. There's a 50% chance it either came premade from the grocery store or it was homemade. There is however a 100% chance it was made about four or five days ago. We were going to throw it away, but then we heard you were coming over. If we can't pawn the rest of it off on you, we'll toss it in the trash right after you leave.

Debra: "Are you *sure* you don't want another piece, Maria?"

"A Brownie"

All the previous statements said about "cake" also apply here. And I hope you like walnuts.

Debra: "Nut allergies? Back in my day, no one was allergic to nuts. If you were allergic, we would have known five minutes ago, Maria." ***No response*** "Maria? Maria?!"

"A Cookie"

To try and not write a full chapter on "What to expect about the cookie," I'm going to try and keep these sentiments short, sweet, and to the point.

#1 – Every Minnesotan is proud of their homemade cookies, and we arguably make the best in the entire country. Therefore, you might visit on the day we just finished baking a fresh batch. Heck, we may have even made them just because of you. Isn't that Minnesota Nice? This also, unfortunately, comes with the burden that if we do offer you one, you are expected to take it, even if it's not your preferred taste. But at the same time, your limit is two. Grandchildren get three, but the third cookie only comes after they finish their dinner.

> Debra: "I'm glad you like the cookie, Maria. It's my mother's recipe. Would you like some coffee to go with it?"

> Maria: "I'll take a glass of milk if you have it."

Debra: "I didn't offer you milk. I offered you coffee."

#2 – If it's a store-bought cookie, expect the cookie is one of the following: a fudge graham, a shortbread cookie with chocolate drizzle, or the store brand "Oreo," which, of course, is a chocolate cookie sandwich accompanied by their pitiful, neglected counterpart: the vanilla cookie sandwich.

Debra: "Would you like an 'Oreo' to go with your coffee?"

Maria: *Squints at the pattern pressed into the cookies and knows instantly they are not 'Oreos' as advertised. The jar contains two chocolate cookie sandwiches amidst about two hundred abandoned vanilla cookie sandwiches. She happily takes the final two chocolate ones* "Thank you."

Debra: "Oh, darn it." *Mood instantly drops as she regrets not taking her choice first. Wishes Maria would have been kind enough to consider a choice of all vanilla or being kind enough to do a one-and-one combination.*

#3 –These are your offerings here in the 21st century. If this was the year 1995 or before, there's a 70% chance the store-bought cookie was a "Fig Newton" and a much higher chance that, yes, it was also the store brand.

Debra: "I grew up on these little delights. Have you had them before? Would you like one?"

Maria: "Are they softer than the candy?"

"Lunch/Dinner"

So, here's the thing. About twice a year, there may be a visit that is going so well that an impromptu meal will occur, and you as the guest will be invited to stay. But the other 99.9% of the time, your invitation to a meal was already pre-planned. Therefore, your contribution to the meal should not have only been expected but also pre-planned.

Yes, we will respect (or silently disapprove) of your freedom to choose whatever you'd like to bring, but the fact is, in addition to having anxiety on whether you're smart enough to even know you should bring something, we are fretting over what item you have chosen to contribute.

The worst thing in the world all Minnesotans fear is that you are bringing something which needs to be prepared once you arrive. You need the microwave to heat up your contribution before it's served? Sure, not a problem. But if you ever have to utter the phrase "Do you have a cutting board?" or "Could I trouble you for a bowl and measuring cups?" or the most sinister of all "Is your oven already on?", don't be surprised if, during the meal prep, conversations begin to die down, or we turn on the TV to *Wheel of Fortune* with a volume louder than what is customary.

> <u>Maria</u>: ***Trying to hear herself think*** "Can you turn the T.V. down, please?"

> <u>Debra</u>: "You requested the use of my oven during the heat wave in July? The lower I turn down the TV volume, the lower I turn down the oven temperature. You choose, Maria. The fate of your enchiladas is in your hands."

"A Phone Call"

You need to make a call? On my landline in the 21st century? It's local, right?

> <u>Debra</u>: ***Listens to the tones of each button as Maria enters the numbers on her landline*** "I think that was more than seven numbers…" ***Grits teeth as she knew she should have offered instant coffee***

I want to stress that everyone involved in these scenarios is still alive and well, and no one suffered a heart attack or needed treatment for anxiety after these encounters. Pat, Debra, and even Maria are very happy in the state of Minnesota (and the state of mind it takes to be in it). Their stories, like many others, are legendary and passed down from generation to generation within the writings and conversations of multiple authors and commentators throughout the Midwest and usually at least one pamphlet found at a county-sponsored rest area.

Maria invites many family members and friends to the town she now calls "home." But before they picnic in Camden State Park, visit AJ's Family Arcade, or taste every Schwan's ice cream flavor, she gives them the lowdown on how to do Minnesota right.

BOOK BREAK!

And now… an opinion on winter:

It's damn too cold for too damn long.

(I can use the word "damn" instead of "darn"
because I'm talking about winter.)

RELIGION: A SPOTLIGHT ON CHRISTIANITY

Oh, religion! If you're worried about finding it or losing it, don't worry—it will always be there. That is one nice thing I can say about most churches throughout the state: the door is always open... unless they locked it. We take religion seriously just like any other state, but "Minnesota Nice" adds a clear resin coating on top that says: judgments of religion should be seen and not heard. What exactly does this mean?

Here's an example: If you're on a first date in the Deep South, at some point you're going to get asked "Which church do you go to?" At first glance, this may not appear to be a problem. But consider the implications of this question:

#1 It assumes you are indeed religious and are not questioning your faith, or worse, a nonbeliever.

#2 It assumes you care about church just as much as the person asking. This isn't the time to tell them you only go to the Easter and Christmas Eve service each year.

Why do they want to know "which" church? If you think there *isn't* a wrong answer to this question, you are severely mistaken.

How does this compare to Minnesota? I'm not going to ask you which church you go to on the first date. Well, unless we have a good feeling the date's gonna end up in the bedroom. After all, I want to know if you're going to shout out "Oh, Jesus!" or "Oh, Mr. Goldstein!" ahead of time.

No, if Minnesotans wished we had any sixth sense at all, it would be to just look someone dead in the eye and use some x-ray vision to see which religion they follow and the last time they attended services. Unfortunately, none of us possess that power. So, we do what Minnesotans do: we judge silently as self-proclaimed experts...

1. Nike shoes? Catholic!

2. Sketchers? Protestant!

3. Adidas? Muslim!

4. Gold Buckles? Jewish!

5. Crocs? Doesn't matter! They've already sold their soul to Satan.

At the risk of being labeled a person who not only casts judgment upon others by writing this, but also a person who imposes absolutes, I will use the wisdom of my Spanish Teacher and Speech Coach (thank you, Mrs. P.) by saying, "Never say never and never say always because you're very rarely right." Do silent judgmental people exist in the South? Of course, they do! Do loud judgmental people exist in the North? Of course, they do! Do loud judgmental people exist in Minnesota? ...Would you like a cup of coffee?

Many locations across the United States have recognized that attendance for organized services has declined as younger generations feel empowered to make their own decisions. (Regret telling Millennials "You can be whatever you want to be" during their formative years yet?) One unexpected consequence of this was the revelation that showing up to the House of God (by any name) at 8 a.m. was too much to bear after staying up until 3 a.m. watching YouTube videos grandma wouldn't approve of. On a related note, fast-paced technology has been a difficult challenge for organized religion to keep up with. After all, hearing a ten-minute message from a monotone speaker who accidentally spits on congregates sitting in the front row describing what the apocalypse looks like won't ever compare to a simple Facebook meme showing Jesus Christ hugging a crying dinosaur and holding a lightsaber—delivering the exact same message.

But, in the end, I'm always reminded of the wisdom my own religious sponsor gave me when I was 11 years old after I revealed to him my fears of our own church not surviving the downward shift in attendance: have faith. After all, God and the offering plate will always find a way.

Randy & Linda Wright
St. Cloud, Minnesota

Randy and Linda are young newlyweds who just moved into suburbia. Randy just received a big promotion at Wells Fargo Bank, which means Linda just received a higher spending limit on their credit card. Their relationship carries an interesting dynamic since Randy has retained his conservative upbringing, and Linda has retained all her Beanie Babies from childhood. Her most recent accomplishment was the adoption of a stray cat—which Randy says only shows up when his wife leaves cat food and milk on the back porch.

As mentioned above, this couple is also an example of how religion might not be in the forefront of their minds compared to their parents' generations. However, they decided to try and put their best foot forward and continue the tradition of their Minnesota upbringing while adjusting to culture and practice of the 21st century.

"Christian"

Minnesotans are always up for the challenge of defining what a Christian is. It must be that ancient Puritan blood which rears its head on the full moon and tells us we're experts on the subject for the simple fact that we've lived. Unfortunately, problems arise immediately when sharing your characteristics of a Christian. Essentially, once you've declared your first one, immediately understand that you have failed, and you are indeed going to Hell. But let's give this exercise a shot, shall we?

> Linda: "You know, I think, to be a good Christian, you need to be a good person."
>
> Randy: "What is a 'good' person, Linda? By whose definition? And for how long? Nobody saw it—does it still count? Can I have a cheat day? Can I double up on a Friday so I can avoid being 'good' on Saturday?"
>
> Linda: "Bad day at work?"
>
> Randy: "No. The Twins lost."
>
> Linda: ***Nods*** "Every time…"

Then, there are my two favorite Minnesota characteristics:

> Linda: "Oh, gosh darn it, did I just sin? Well, as long as *I* feel bad on the inside, that's what counts."
>
> Randy: "Did you hear what happened to the neighbor's house? Burned down to the ground. Really sad. Linda should make them a hot dish. Or maybe she can bake them some blueberry muffins. I bet she'll go over and help them

clean up. Wish there was something *I* could do.
I know! I'll keep them in my thoughts."

However, one sure way you know you've run into a Minnesotan Christian is the fact someone will tell you how someone *else* felt you failed in the eyes of the Lord. And, like always, I'll go ahead and share directly what it is Minnesotans are thinking. Because without me, you were going to have to suffer three layers of neighbors bearing false witness to get this truth:

Naming your child "Christian" is one of the most arrogant, self-righteous moves which guarantees he's going to grow up to be an asshole. And don't get me started on the name "Nevaeh." If you think reversing the letters in "heaven" for your child's name is paying homage to God—just remember that one of the most common signs an individual is possessed by Satan is the innate ability to recite words backward like it's a common language. Now, everybody, in a Rob Zombie voice shout "NE-VA-EH!"

Hmm. That was a rant. A long rant. Kind of like a sermon... Will the ushers please pass around the offering plates?

"Sermon"

Speaking of sermons, ever wonder how Minnesotans practice "Minnesota Nice" and build up their strength to withstand the lengthy monologue?

> Randy: *Whispers* "Why is the pastor talking about the day their childhood dog was hit by a car and they found it dead in the ditch? What does this have to with the miracle of God?"

> Linda: *Whispers back* "I ... don't know. To be honest, I'm only half paying attention. Maybe

it's an Easter resurrection thing? It's that time of year, you know."

<u>Randy</u>: "It's July."

<u>Linda</u>: "Oh. Right. Maybe it's a patriotic thing."

Don't get me wrong. I'm not here to tell you Minnesota churches are boring. But there's a reason why, if you wanna experience a service that makes you feel the spirit and shout at the top of your lungs "Praise the Lord!" as your heart palpitates and forehead sweats (from the lack of air conditioning), you go to the South! You know what's not the South? Minnesota. As a matter of fact, you can't go any farther north in the contiguous United States. The odds say you aren't going to feel the urge to jump to your feet that entire hour of service unless your leg falls asleep.

So, in preparation of that, Randy and Linda bring a few things with them that I think you will find most helpful:

- A preferred flavor of chewing gum (Nicorette if you're trying to quit smoking—A.K.A.—this is NOT the time to test Day One.)
- A Werther's Original butterscotch candy
- A pen and pad for a discreet game of Tic-Tac-Toe

- Water to drink (sanctification not required—it wouldn't save you from hearing the ten-minute sermon anyway)
- A 60" flat screen TV with surround sound for the kickoff of the NFL game you're missing.
- The mindset you're already better than the neighbor who didn't show up for service—You go, Randy!

And finally, Randy brings an extra $20 he'll inevitably fork over into the offering plate because it is way too obvious to everyone that he didn't cope well today. It's okay. He'll overdramatically toss President Jackson face up on top of all the other offerings just so everyone within judging distance knows he did it. Finally, he'll nod at the parishioner next to him.

> Randy: *Grins to himself and silently communicates* "See that $20? Yeah, that's right. I did that."

"The Bible"

If you're from Minnesota, odds are you have at least one in the bottom of a drawer somewhere in the house... unless it got lost in the move.

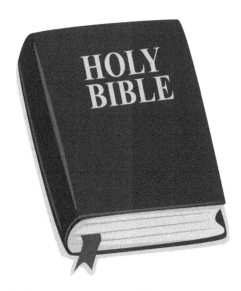

> Randy: "Linda... I'm asking where you put the Bible!"

> Linda: "I promise! It's around here somewhere!"

A spiritual side table decoration which regrettably indicates the last time you dusted.

> Linda: "Oh, jeez! Haven't done *that* in a while."

The Good Book is still available in some hotel rooms and the only item which won't glow when the room lights go out and the "black light" goes on.

> Randy: "That just tells you how pure Jesus really is."

But what Minnesotans appreciate the most is the Bible's countless accommodations:

- "Too heavy to pick up? Now in travel size!"
- "Too ugly to look at? Now in purple!"
- "Too many words to read? Now abridged!"
- "Too difficult to read? Now with pictures!"
- "Too stupid to read? Now a TV series!"
- "Too boring to watch? Now in a musical!"
- "Too hard to get through? Look, I've given you enough options. If it doesn't work, then maybe you *should* go to Hell… Michigan! Take a spiritual journey and then try the list again."

"Church"

In Minnesota, it's not a matter of "if"; it's a matter of "what time and which place." It doesn't mean you're showing up. But it *is* expected you know when services are offered by heart just like your phone number or address.

> Randy: "My wife and I regularly attend…" *Pauses* "Our Lady of Hope—"
>
> Linda: "—Our Lady of Grace."
>
> Randy: "It has services every Sunday at 11 a.m."
>
> Linda: "The services are at 10."
>
> Randy: "The preacher—"

Linda: "—The pastor"

Randy: "He's—"

Linda: "—She's…"

Randy: "Very nice."

Keep in mind, for a third of the white population who attends services, this is their only social life and the only time their albino skin sees sunlight. So, if you thought the entire ordeal was only going to last an hour—I'm here to give you another Minnesota revelation. There's going to be a 30-minute tearful Minnesota reunion before the actual service… with coffee. And then, there's going to be a 30-minute tearful Minnesota goodbye after the service… with coffee and bars.

Randy: "And this was the day God rested?"

Minneapolis and St. Paul feature some very beautiful churches built on the backs of many men like Randy who also have guilt-donated an extra $20 after realizing a Minnesota church service is a two-hour experience instead of one. But you must remember, most of Minnesota is made up of small country towns. A majority of churches are very conservative in composition and style. It's the people there that give it that memorable stain—I mean, touch—I mean, lasting impression.

Linda: "Randy, this Lutefisk supper is a *fundraiser* for the church to fix the leak in the roof."

Randy: "But it says, 'Free Will Donation.' I already gave my weekly $20."

Linda: "That's not what 'Free Will Donation' means. It means God is 'free to will you' to donate."

Randy: ***Sigh*** "There goes another $5."

Linda: ***Gives a stern look and whispers*** "The Johnsons before us gave a $20."

Randy: "Okay... $10."

"Catholic"

Please read the following disclaimers which will come from a "Devout Catholic" Service:

The early exposure to Communion and precursor to your child's later struggle with alcoholism *(Just knock it back quick, Timmy!)*

Knee and joint pain from constant kneeling *(All in the name of Jesus.)*

Receiving gifts (Donations required first.)

Priests who ask—and expect you to answer *(Lord have mercy.)*

The claustrophobic sensation of unscented candles burning *(Forever and ever, Amen.)*

Forgiveness and everlasting love (Non-member experience may differ.)

Randy: "My mother wanted me to stay Catholic after we got married but—"

Linda: "—But we had a discussion and mutual agreement that switching to Protestant was a better move. Didn't we, Randy?"

Randy: "…My mother wasn't too happy."

Linda: "We don't have to worry about that anymore. She died last year."

Randy: ***Looks around the living room*** "Where's the urn with her ashes?"

Linda: "With the Bible."

Randy: "With the Bible we can't find?"

"Lutheran"

Under the diverse branch of Protestants, or what Catholics call "traitors," you will find a large sect who call themselves "Lutheran" named after Martin Luther himself. (No, not the black guy. But wouldn't it be cool if it were?)

If people stopped caring about religion, then actor Joseph Fiennes would be completely out of a job. Either that or put him in a movie about Evolution. The genre could be called "Religious Horror."

Even within the Lutheran faith itself, there are two large branches: E.L.C.A. & Missouri-Synod. To help separate the two, I say this: One will invite you to church and give you a 'Thank You' card as you leave. The other will invite you to church and give you a list of "suggested" changes you could make before coming back.

Randy: "The membership form is asking for all of our income and investment accounts. Are you sure we should do this?"

Linda: "It's what God would have asked for, Randy."

Please read the following disclaimers which will come from a "Good Lutheran" service:

A live musical *(Let's sing a reprisal of Hymn #178.)*

Grape juice communion (Because that's what Jesus would have done.)

Coffee prelude (*I can get through this!*)

Coffee intermission (*I'm not going to make it!*)

Coffee post-service *(I made it! Now I get a bar for dessert! Oh hell, who put nuts in this?!)*

"Methodists, Presbyterians, Baptists, Pentecostals, Adventists, Jehovah's Witnesses, Mormons"

<u>Linda</u>: "The 'other' Protestants? ***Thinks to self*** They're around here somewhere. I'll inquire about them in a bit, but I'm still looking for my Bible. Randy, did you look in the moving box marked 'Miscellaneous'?"

"The Church Basement"

Protestants love a church basement because it's a social gathering place where they commit their first sin post-services by gossiping. At least, there's coffee.

<u>Any Lutheran</u>: "Did you hear what the neighbor said?!"

Catholics hate basements because it puts you 20 feet closer to Hell of which I am told is somewhere between the Mantle and Outer Crust of Earth's layers. This is why Catholics prefer balconies—it is also where they commit their sin *during* the service by gossiping.

<u>Any Catholic</u>: "Did you hear what the Pope said?!"

"Non-Denominational Service"

Years ago, a "Non-denominational Service" simply meant it was an open invitation for all to come in to share and express their faith. Typically, this open invitation happened once or twice a year to help acquire new membership. Since the rise of Mega-churches, the term itself has morphed into its own system with its own dedication location.

<u>Randy</u>: "A 'nondenominational' service? But... that means they're still Catholic, right?"

<u>Linda</u>: "Look at the size of this place! These non-denominational churches look like convention centers!"

<u>Randy</u>: "I wonder how they stay in business?"

<u>Linda</u>: "Hey! They got a Starbucks here!"

<u>Randy</u>: "Question answered."

Now, if only, during communion, the "Body of Christ" was a slice of a Minnesotan blueberry muffin and the "Blood of Christ" was a shot of Mocha Iced Coffee. I mean, I'd thank Jesus for sacrificing himself for *that!*

"Minnesota Vikings"

It doesn't matter if you're Catholic, Protestant, or even a Christian. Following this team is considered a religion in itself. All Minnesotans can agree on the following when it comes to the Vikings...

- Skol
- Purple & Gold
- Maybe this time...

For those of you NOT from Minnesota... I will do some clarifying...

- <u>Skol</u> – we did not misspell the word "School"—it means "Cheers!" with [preferably] a beer.
- <u>Purple & Gold</u> – represents the team colors. (Across the state, we're glad Barney the Dinosaur and the Teletubbies aren't a thing anymore.)
- <u>"Maybe this time..."</u> – The Vikings keep telling us if we as a state continue to vote for the losing presidential candidate in the primaries, they'll win a Super Bowl. *(The Vikings have yet to hold up their end of the bargain.)*

CHRISTIAN   JUDAIC   ISLAM   HINDU   BUDDHIST

A final comment I'd like to add is I'm very aware that other religions are alive and well in Minnesota: Judaism, Muslim, Taoism, Republican, and many more. I will say it loud and say it proud: You exist, and I see you. (Which is more than I can say for Randy's mother's ashes.)

BOOK BREAK!

And now... a misconception on rural folk:

No—we do NOT drive tractors and
lawn mowers to school!
...Most of us don't.

THE GREAT OUTDOORS

Red pine
Pinus resinosa

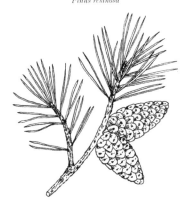

O ne thing to point out is a newbie to the state, who also hasn't experienced the Midwest, will find the yearly weather quite the adjustment. For starters, the season of spring is ... hypothetical. If the world didn't settle on an exact date based on the earth's tilt, a Minnesotan wouldn't be able to tell you when spring started nor when it stopped.

When it comes to summer, many outsiders wrongfully think (thanks to another delightful season *cough cough*) the state is blanketed in a cool, dry temperature which makes it *just* pleasant enough to wear shorts and a t-shirt. The fact is: a blistering heat accompanied by hellish humidity consumes most of the state after nature flips a magical switch to declare the *real* arrival of this season. Explaining fall is no different than explaining spring: no one is sure when it arrived, and no one knows when it left.

Of course, the season you all want to hear about is winter. Yes, you already know Minnesota winters are cold, and at some point, the snow will be bountiful and plenty (usually in February and March). After Alaska, Minnesota and North Dakota can be argued as the coldest states in the U.S. In short, the only guarantee we can give you is ... cold will happen, and it will be here long after you've had your fill.

A visual paradise? It certainly has it with any variation a person could want: colorful bluffs in the Southeast, wavy fields in the West, dense woods in the North, lakes and rivers scattered throughout, and road construction everywhere. To me, nothing makes Minnesota feel like home more than finding some sort of connection with nature, whether I'm swimming in a lake during the hot summer, walking a trail in the tepid spring, celebrating the harvest amid the crisp fall, or exploring the wonders and fun of a brisk winter.

John Jackson & Brad Hanson
Warroad, Minnesota

Oh, let me tell ya: you're in for a treat now. This one small town near the Canadian border has a proud and iconic history you would never expect. Whatever is in the water up there, don't expect them to stop drinking it anytime soon. With a population just shy of 2,000 residents, they've birthed over a half dozen Olympians in the sport of hockey. You don't get granted the name "Hockeytown, USA" otherwise. It is a perfect location to help acclimate you to what the outdoors is all about in this state as it sits on the shores of Lake of the Woods, an incomparable landmark itself.

As for the town, the unique name "Warroad" is derived from the Ojibwe tribes who lived there before Europeans occupied the area along with the entire state. The first thing you are going to want to make sure is how to pronounce the town's namesake by its modern locals. Like the lazy pronunciation "Minnesoda" as the locals do, we also decided on the quick sound of "Warrid." Living in the state as I did, this choice intrigues me considering any native Minnesotan gives themselves away by over-pronouncing the word "road" like it's a mile's journey just to reach one. The rule doesn't apply to *this* word.

John is one of the lucky few who was born in this historic town but also one of the *unlucky* few who blew out his knee in a backyard hockey match ten years ago. Thus, after high school, he switched his career path and is honored to work for the Minnesota Department of Natural Resources. Now, despite any misgivings that the MN DNR is really a front designed to stop Canadian refugees from illegally crossing over into the United States, John's goal is really to protect and regulate one of the most important industries there: commercial fishing. Unless the windchill indicates a temperature of zero or below, the pain receptors on the outside of his body died many years ago, and he's fine with just wearing a heavy sweatshirt under a light windbreaker. It's just one of the many signs he's acclimated. After all, shorts weather starts at a balmy 45 degrees.

Brad is John's best friend. He's no stranger to Minnesota as he grew up in Granite Falls. But with the reputation Warroad High School possessed from (you guessed it) hockey, his family moved there his sophomore year to help harness his potential. For the past five years, Brad has enjoyed the accolades of being an Olympian for the sport he loves. The perks are just as prestigious as you'd expect: his name is memorialized at his former high school on a plaque in the hallway closest to the men's bathroom, he receives a priority line boarding pass at the Warroad International Memorial Airport, he gets a secured spot on the fire truck during the yearly Warroad summer parade, and he can count on getting a free beer at Breakers Bar whenever the Minnesota Wild have a good season. Does he wear that Olympic hockey jersey every chance he gets? You bet your ass he does!

"Fishing"

A way of life—God's sport—that thing you do after church on Sunday. Can't make it in person? Watch it on TV!

John: "Brad, wanna go fishin'?"

Brad: "Does a walleye pounce on a Bass Pro rig with a shiner at dawn?"

John: "Not when *you* do it."

Brad: *Adjusts his cap* "You're buying me a six-pack of Michelob for that comment."

"Ice Fishing"

We are grateful for the past time that can be enjoyed 24/7. Plus, it's something to do when the Vikings don't make (or biff) the playoffs.

> Brad: "John, wanna go fishin'?"
>
> John: "Does a muskie pounce on Rapala jig with a shiner at sunset?"
>
> Brad: "Not when *you* do it."
>
> John: ***Adjusts his camo jacket*** "You're buying me a bottle of Flying Dutchman for that comment."

"Ice Skating"

Because you want that hockey scholarship. No. You *need* that hockey scholarship.

Brad: "You got your skates on, and you've been sitting in the lodge for 20 minutes. Why aren't you out on the ice?"

John: "Holy buckets! I just realized I forgot something at home. Haven't seen them for a while neither."

Brad: "What's that?"

John: "My ankles."

"Lakes"

An outdoorsman's paradise; one step closer to heaven; a natural resource; a swimming pool; a guilt-free toilet when needed.

Brad: "Is there anything better than a lake in Minnesota?"

John: "A beer."

Brad: "Is there anything better than a lake and a beer in Minnesota?"

John: "A boat."

Brad: "Is there anything better than a lake, a beer, and a boat in Minnesota?"

John: "A woman by my side."

Brad: "Is there anything better than a lake, a beer, a boat, and a woman by your side in Minnesota?"

John: "A woman by my side who fishes."

Brad: "Is there anything better than a lake, a beer, a boat, and a woman by your side who fishes in Minnesota?"

John: "Can she clean the fish, too?"

Brad: "I wouldn't push your luck, John."

"School Closure/Snow Day"

If you're the first to say it out loud and it *doesn't* happen—you're in deep doo-doo*! (*see "Crap" for "doo-doo" definition)

Brad: "Looks like the kids got out of school because of the snow."

John: ***Shakes head*** "And where is the first place they go after they get out?"

Brad: "Outdoors in the snow."

"Snow"

Yes, we love it. But we were okay with it snowing *tomorrow*. Sorry, skiers, snowmobilers, and ice fishermen. We just need one more day before the gentle snowflakes fall and condense into a rock-hard cement for the next five months.

John: "It snowed three inches last night."

Brad: *Shakes his head in disappointment* "It's not enough."

John: "With the few inches we got last week? How much do you need?"

Brad: "I need more! Don't you understand?! More, more, MORE!"

"Snow-mobiling"

What's a snowmobile? Think of it like a life-sized die-cast Hot Wheels car shaped like a miniature Batmobile with the top down with skis instead of wheels and a throttle. Now, imagine it rolling on top of snow like it's 1990s short-haired carpet. Got it?

Brad: "You sure you wanna try that hill?"

John: "Absolutely! My Polaris sled can handle anything!"

Brad: "But can your ego handle it when you completely biff it?"

"The Common Loon"

This is proudly Minnesota's State Bird. Why a loon for the state accolade? Mainly because a cow doesn't qualify as a bird.

Brad: "Is that the sound of a broken flute or a young kid screaming in pain?"

John: ***Listens in*** "I think it's a loon."

Brad: "Are you talking the 'bird' kind or the 'needs to be committed' kind?"

"Thunderstorms"

Does EVERY thunderstorm have to be declared as a severe weather event? If I have to hear that automated female voice on the radio again, I swear… "Take shelter immediately. Stay indoors and away from winDOWS!"

Brad: ***Prays desperately*** "Lord, don't let it hail, and spare my truck. I parked it under the tree. Maybe it won't be so bad."

John: ***Five minutes later*** "Hmm. 'Fallen branch—meet Tim's truck. Tim's truck—meet fallen branch.'"

"Mosquitos" / "No See-'ems"

Perhaps the only pestilence most Minnesotans have contemplated selling their soul for in exchange for their extinction.

Brad: "Those darn skeeters are after every drop of blood in my body today, Jeez!"

John: "What did you bring for repellent?"

Brad: "Every suggestion I could find on the internet: spray, wipes, gel, pads, soaps, oils, candles, dryer sheets, lights, zappers, traps, smoke bombs, a flame thrower, a giant bat, my firstborn, and a crucifix."

"Hunting"

The right-of-passage for modern hunting usually starts with the gift of a first shotgun on a birthday or Christmas and a class on Gun Safety. We're looking at the average age of 12 when we trust the next generation to shoot their first deer and hopefully not the neighbor's dog.

John: *At the local bar* "Hey! Brad may have his celebrity hockey career, but I still hold our hunting record!"

Bartender: "Oh, yeah? What's your record? A 12-point buck?"

John: "Four of them—right in a row."

<u>Bartender</u>: "Is that even legal?"

<u>Brad</u>: "He's talking about his record on the *Big Buck Hunter* simulator down at the arcade."

<u>John</u>: "My name is still there as the 'Top Scorer.'"

<u>Brad</u>: "At least you correctly listed your initials on the Score Board as 'A.S.S.'"

"Wind"

Here is the driver of most of the weather in the Midwest for any season. The reason? States within this area were failed by our Canadian brethren to the north in offering any man-made or natural protection from the winds originating from the Artic Circle. Minnesota is no different. It does make you wonder if this resentment was the origins of our state's willingness to poke fun and make jokes about our Canadian neighbor to the north. Nah—they just talk funny.

<u>John</u>: "You got that 'red' look."

<u>Brad</u>: "How?"

<u>John</u>: "Your cheeks are red. I suppose it's from the wind."

<u>Brad</u>: "If only that darn wind would stop, it'd be a nice day out."

<u>John</u>: ***Checks outside*** "Hey, I think it did. It's barely a breeze now."

<u>Brad</u>: "Great! Now if only that darn temperature wasn't so cold, it'd be a nice day out."

"Hockey"

It's played indoors and it's played outdoors. Jason Voorhees from the movie series *Friday the 13th* may be the iconic one with the mask, but Minnesota is the expert on the stick and the puck.

<u>Brad</u>: "Did I ever tell you the story of when I—"

<u>John</u>: "—got out of the penalty box in the last 30 seconds of the game during the Olympic finals and scored the winning goal? Nope. But I can't wait to hear it." ***Chugs the rest of his beer as he contemplates his own life's accomplishments***

"Camping"

This is the quintessential pastime you need to experience here in the great state of Minnesota. The idea itself encompasses so many enjoyable activities that you are sure to make many happy memories: bocce ball, ladder golf, swimming, boating, jet skis, fishing, campfires, horseshoes, trails, grill-outs, bean bags, Tiki Torches, camper lights, lawn chairs, and (if it rains all weekend) the origins of that positive pregnancy test.

John: "All right, I packed my tent, sleeping bag, pillow, water-free body wash, a light jacket, battery-operated lamp, camp stove, a cooler, lawn chair, and my fishing gear. And I even brought my own toilet paper just in case. What did you bring, Brad?"

Brad: "My 5th wheel pull-behind camper complete with full-sized bedroom and mattress, private shower and bathroom, gas stove, fully stocked mini-fridge, microwave, dining room/ living room combo, bike rack, extra storage, and surround sound speakers."

John: "Uff-da! I thought you said we were 'roughin' it' this weekend?!"

Brad: "We are! I left the portable satellite dish at home. Hopefully we can get the Twins game on the radio."

"Memorial Day Weekend"

You *say* it's the start of summer, but this 30-degree weather says otherwise.

> <u>John</u>: "It's snowing? I'm on vacation at the end of May; why is it snowing?!"

Even though it may seem contradictory, John and Brad have had many fulfilling experiences here throughout the state. Their friendship and the town they live in truly make each season unique and special and are the reasons they keep doing it all again. When you leave Minnesota, you always find your way back, don't cha know?

BOOK BREAK!

And now... a truth about our neighboring states:

We don't hate you. We tease, make jokes, and form rivalries for light-hearted fun. You are all still eligible to receive "Minnesota Nice." Even Wisconsin.*

*In-person experience not guaranteed.

PLACES

SAINT PAUL
MINNESOTA

My favorite places? Man, there are so many. I have great childhood memories of skipping basalt rocks, harvesting wild blueberries, eating crawdads, and being chased by angry wasps near the north shore. I saw a wonderful performance of *A Doll's House* at the Guthrie Theater in downtown Minneapolis. It truly made up for needing to call the tow company in order to get my car back. (A word to the wise: Minneapolis is very protective of their streets—especially ones labeled with "No parking here" signs.) Haunted Hayrides in the state were always a joy. Minnesota doesn't hold back when it comes to being spooky. And there's simply no comparison when it comes to a man jumping out of a corn-field dressed as Dracula trying to scare you in his Minnesotan accent. "I want to suck your blood, ya? Is that okay?"

But my favorite place to be as a kid was at a local camp-ground near a great fishing lake. Where I live now just doesn't offer the same experience I crave to relive from childhood. I can still hear my mother say in that loud, authoritative tone whenever the fishing trip was done: "You catch 'em, you clean 'em!" Little did I know that wisdom would also be applicable years later to my dating life. Thanks, mom.

But there are so many more places throughout the state than what I grew up experiencing. Our next segment here sadly doesn't introduce you to any more natives or visitors considering the topics will cover many different places and times. But don't let that discourage you! Our existing volunteers will happily walk you through several noteworthy places. After reading, I strongly encourage you to research and discover on your own the wonder that is our state.

"Anoka, Minnesota"

Known as the "Halloween Capital of the World" due to a full city effort in organizing a Halloween Party to promote safe celebrations. To be fair, most events on October 31st are safe in Minnesota. Why? Because no one wants to commit a crime during a snowstorm. Blizzard of 1991, anyone?

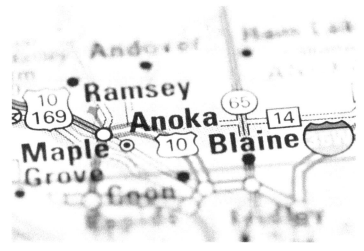

Alice: "Remember when we pulled our kids in the sleds across the neighbor's yard to go Trick-or-Treating?"

Hank: "I pulled the sleds; you drank the amaretto coffee. Did you think that was fair?"

Alice: "Of course, I do. It was Halloween. You got the trick, and I got the treat."

"Chanhassen, Minnesota"

When we say we love art in Minnesota, that means we LOVE art in Minnesota. One of the finest examples is the historic Chanhassen Dinner Theater, which has been running since 1968 and claims to be the largest, private dinner theater company in the nation.

If that doesn't convince you about the love we have for art, we also gave birth to a prince. And not just any prince, *the* Prince. Prince Rogers Nelson was born here in Chanhassen. Since the 1980s, we've proudly drove red Corvettes, worn raspberry berets, and danced in purple rain.

Jane: "Where were you on December 31ˢᵗ 1999?"

Jane's mother: "The Holiday Inn in downtown Mankato partying like it was 1999."

Charlie: "But it *was* still 1999. What did you need to party 'like it' for?"

Jane's mother: "You had to be there at the hotel to know."

Charlie: "I wasn't there."

Jane's mother: "That's why it was good time."

"Duluth, Minnesota"

Duluth itself represents a lot of what Minnesota has to offer regarding its natural resources. It is a port city to the largest of the Great Lakes: Lake Superior. What was once a major fur trade location in the 1800s turned into one of the vital iron ore ports in the nation from the once booming Iron Range in the 1900s. Today, it is a busy tourist location for both the city and state alike.

John: "Brad, you should read this! According to this, back in the 1800s, Duluth used to have tons of beaver just out on display in the store-front windows! You could even purchase them! Man, I wish they still did that today."

Brad: "You're thinking of the Red-Light District in Amsterdam. That's not the same kind of beaver they're talking about here."

"Bars/Taverns/Saloons"

<approximately every five miles or every third city block>

The most popular gathering place in the state, second only to church (or so they'd have you believe). Contrary to the venue's historically negative reputation, here in this state, it is the ideal place for any occasion: after-work gathering, birthday, casual dinner, graduation party, sporting event viewing party, anniversary, engagement party, wedding reception, marriage consummation, the birth, the baptism, before the funeral, after the funeral, or during the funeral if you were told not to attend the service.

Linda: "I haven't been to this bar in ages!"

Randy: "It's hard to find a good beer worth the price at a bar these days. Back in his day, my dad said there was an early bird special at his favorite bar. Beer on tap started at a quarter and went up twenty-five cents every 30 minutes until happy hour was over. They don't do stuff like that anymore."

Linda: "Are you done ranting?"

Randy: "Yeah."

Linda: "Do you need anything right now?"

Randy: "A brewski."

Linda: "They're $7.00 here."

Randy: "It's a dollar cheaper at the bar next door. Let's go."

"Best Buy"

<Headquarters @ Richfield, Minnesota>

In the 1990s and early 2000s, this company exploded in popularity, overtaking Radio Shack for all your electronic needs and competing with Wal-Mart and Target for your entertainment needs regarding movies, music, and video games. This is also a Minnesota-based company originally founded under the name "Sound of Music" before expanding and rebranding to "Best Buy" in 1983.

Charlie: "I'm here to pick-up my new TV from my online order."

Best Buy Clerk: "I'm sorry, sir. Your order is actually in Maple Grove."

Charlie: "But I ordered it here in Hopkins."

Best Buy Clerk: "No, you actually tried ordering it at the Eden Prairie location, but they were out of stock. So, it was rerouted to Maple Grove."

Charlie: "Can't you just reroute the order here to the Hopkins store?"

Best Buy Clerk: "I'm sorry, sir. You're going to have to call the Eden Prairie store, tell them to stop the order in Maple Grove, then call and confirm Maple Grove has taken your name off the order so that when you reorder here, you don't get charged for two TVs. Then, you will need to call your credit card company to make sure they block the prior authorization on the first order but make sure they allow the prior authorization on the second order. I would then call the Hopkins location here to make sure we have it in stock; otherwise, we'll reroute it back to Maple Grove."

"Blue Earth, Minnesota"

The city's location is the center point of the construction for Interstate I-90, which was simultaneously being built eastward from Seattle, Washington, and westward from Boston, Massachusetts. The accomplishment is often compared to the Transcontinental Railroad and parallels many aspects of its construction. In 1978, Blue Earth was so proud of its accolade, they commemorated the event by painting the road gold as a nod to the gold spike used to finalize the railroad's construction in 1869.

The Jolly Green Giant canning company was so significant, Blue Earth built a 55.5-foot tall statue that can be seen prominently while driving across the city on either Highway 169 or Interstate I-90. Visitors over the age of 18 wonder why the attraction doesn't have more entertainment value. Visitors under the age of 18 wonder if the Giant is wearing underwear. (Look straight up to find out!)

> Randy: "The statue is great, but I kinda thought the gift shop would have been bigger."
>
> Linda: *Smiles as she looks up the giant's "leaf cloth"* "Oh, it's big enough."
>
> Randy: *In shock* "Linda, stop that! People can see you from the road!"
>
> Linda: "Oh, this reminds me... I need peas and a carrot for tonight's dinner."
>
> Randy: *Evaluates comment* "What do you mean 'a carrot'?"

Linda: "When you find one big enough, that's all you need."

"Caribou Coffee"

<Headquarters @ Minneapolis, Minnesota>

In 1992, the city of Edina birthed Caribou Coffee. The lore and myth of its origins comes from John Puckett and his wife Kim taking a trip to Alaska. I think Kim either kissed a caribou or John ran over one with a truck? Either way, Kim raised enough funds to start the very first coffee shop and honored the Alaskan animal as its mascot. Take that, Starbucks!

Charlie: "Now, *this* is good coffee!"

Jane's mother: "It's always better when someone else pays for it."

Charlie: "What?"

Jane's mother: "I said 'Daybreak Blend,' please."

"General Mills"

<Headquarters @ Minneapolis, Minnesota>

If you couldn't guess from the name, the company founded in 1866 was originally a flour mill. Gold Medal flour, Betty Crocker syrup, Yoplait yogurt, Nature Valley crunch bars, and Totino's pizza rolls accompany some of our favorite cereal brands: Cheerios, Chex, Lucky Charms, Trix, and Cocoa Puffs.

Maria: ***While stocking the shelves*** "How come we don't stock Frosted Flakes or Raisin Bran in the store? They're my son's favorites."

Pat: "Did she just talk about that 'other' company?"

Maria: "What 'other' company?"

Debra: "Kellogg's. That's a Michigan company, not a Minnesota company."

Maria: ***Confused*** "Forgive me?"

Debra: "Go easy on her, Pat. She didn't know."

"Hormel"

<Headquarters @ Austin, Minnesota>

Those outside the Midwest may not immediately recognize Black Label bacon under the name Hormel. But the company itself has gone beyond the status of supplying pork-based products. Under the parent company, you will also find Dinty Moore, Jennie-O, Planters, Skippy, and Spam.

Randy: "I'm home. What's for dinner?"

Linda: "Soup. Vegetable beef."

Randy: "Yum! I haven't had homemade vegetable beef soup in years."

Linda: "It's not homemade. Even better—it's Dinty Moore."

Randy: ***Long pause*** "Better, huh?"

Linda: "Absolutely!" ***Enthusiastically*** "And if you look in the back of the book you're reading, you'll find a coupon for your next purchase of—"

Randy: "No, no! We can't do that."

"The R. W. Lindholm Service Station"

< Cloquet, Minnesota>

Frank Lloyd Wright has many design accolades to his name: The Guggenheim Museum, The Westcott House, The Unity Temple, The Annunciation Greek Orthodox Church, and The Imperial Hotel. Did the R. W. Lindholm Service Station situated in Cloquet, Minnesota, not come to mind as one of his most notable creations? We'd forgive you it if it didn't. It was supposed to be the genesis of the utopian Broadacre City designed by the ambitious architect. Unfortunately, that vision never came to pass.

> Brad: "Why on earth would anyone want to use a gas station designed by Frank Lloyd Wright?"
>
> John: "What's wrong with that? He's one of the most famous and accomplished architects of his time."
>
> Brad: "I don't want to walk into a gas station bathroom designed by Frank Lloyd Wright. Toilets on the floors, toilets on the walls, and toilets on the ceiling hanging upside down."
>
> John: "That's not Frank Lloyd Wright. You're thinking of a bathroom designed by M.C. Escher."

"Land O' Lakes"

<Headquarters@ Arden Hills, Minnesota>

Anyone who went to a grocery store and wasn't lactose intolerant could tell you what the picture of the female Indian in the dairy section was advertising: Land O' Lakes butter. The depiction of Ojibwe Indian "Mia" unfortunately underwent several changes until her presence was completely diminished in 2020, but she will never be forgotten.

Hank: "I don't understand the issue. How can Native Americans be offended by having one of their own proudly displayed on an American product?"

Alice: "Mia was always portrayed as a primitive character who always wore traditional clothing. The native community thought it promoted her as only a surface stereotype."

Hank: "In 2020, Native Americans were offended the picture had her in traditional clothing? Why?"

Alice: "In 2020, can you name an American company who proudly uses depictions of white colonists telling Native Americans to 'stay off their land' as their logo?"

Hank: "No."

Alice: "That's why."

"Mall of America"

\<Bloomington, Minnesota\>

Before the turn of the century, one could say the phrase, "I'm going to the mall," and it meant you were going to a local destination. As malls continue to slowly cease their existence, saying the phrase means one place: the Mall of America in Minneapolis. Mothers loved it for the stores, Dads hated it for its parking, and the kids only wanted to see Camp Snoopy. (After licensing negotiations fell through with the *Peanuts* name, the park was rebranded to *Nickelodeon Universe* in 2008.)

Pat: "The Mall of America? It's way too big. You won't find me there."

Debra: "Why not?"

Pat: "We own a general store, Deb. What could you possibly need up there you couldn't get here?"

Maria: "Non-general items?"

Debra: "Exactly!"

Pat: "Nah. We got everything anyone could need. Maria, I need you to put the BOGO sign on the $5 perfume and then dust off the Twinkies and sardine cans."

"Mayo Clinic"

<Headquarters @Rochester, Minnesota >

Originated by William W. Mayo & his sons William J. Mayo and Charles H. Mayo, and best known for its groundbreaking and world-renowned care. Patients are told they come first, doctors are held in the highest regard, and the rest of the employees are told they'll never get parking privileges.

Alice: "Hank, you had that heart procedure done in Rochester at Mayo last year. What did you think?"

Hank: ***Reflects*** "It went well. I enjoyed the care, the stay, and the nurses. But I could have done without the séance."

Alice: "The séance?"

Hank: "I think it was a séance. I just remember them all holding hands and brainstorming how to improve communication skills and team-work. They had a goal chart, star stickers, and everything."

Alice: "And? How did that go?"

Hank: "Successful. I was told the celebratory potluck was at noon."

"Minneapolis, Minnesota/ St. Paul, Minnesota"

The locals refer to it by its nicknames "The Cities" or "Twin Cities." Combined, both locations are known for visual arts, pro-sports, dramatic skylines, proud theater, stellar restaurants, and a hub for craft beer.

Brad: "Can't believe it's your first time coming to The Cities. Are you excited?"

John: "Absolutely. My first in-person Minnesota Wild game? It's a dream come true."

Brad: "Hmm. Traffic today is congested and we're running a bit late. Hopefully this clears up soon."

John: "Don't worry! Google Maps has us taking a short detour on the highway. We'll get there in no time."

Brad: "Which highway?"

John: "Interstate 494."

Brad: "We are so fu—"

"Minnesota State Fair"

<Saint Paul, Minnesota >

4-H, Art, Butter sculptures, Food, Livestock, and a "Princess Kay of the Milky Way" Pageant. Set in late August each year, it claims to be the largest state fair by daily attendance.

Charlie: "What are we standing in line for again?"

Jane: "Sweet Martha's Cookie Jar."

Charlie: "How long are we willing to wait?"

Jane: "When we finally get to the fresh baked cookies, I'll let you know."

"Pillsbury"

<Headquarters @Minneapolis, Minnesota>

That's right! Our Poppin' Fresh Pillsbury Doughboy can call himself a Minnesotan. Since 1965, the kitchen sidekick has been one of the most successful and recognizable mascots for home products. And who can forget that giggle when you push on his non-existent belly button? "Hoo-hoo!"

Hank: "I personally don't understand it. The Doughboy is a kid. And then you have this unknown adult hand reach out and touch him? He's not even wearing clothes."

Alice: "Stop ruining a good thing, Hank."

"Target"

<Headquarters @Minneapolis, Minnesota >

Unless you are from the state, odds are you didn't care to do any research on the fact the headquarters is in Minneapolis, Minnesota. In short, if we couldn't get it at Wal-Mart, we found ourselves sauntering to the nearest Target and rolled our eyes that the same product was 50 cents more.

Jane's mother: "I love Target!"

Charlie: "Why?"

Jane's mother: "They have that cute dog named 'Bullseye.'"

Charlie: "I'm still shopping at Wal-Mart!"

Jane's mother: "Why? They don't have a dog for their mascot. Who do they have?"

Charlie: "They have 'Gary—The Wal-Mart Shopper'!"

Jane's mother: "Isn't that the guy with the ripped jeans-shorts who didn't wear underwear and used a garbage bag as a shirt?"

Charlie: "Yup. 'Merica!"

"The Boundary Waters"

<Ask Rand McNally where it is>

A natural water barrier between our great state and Canada. An absolute beautiful site and a location a U.S. President never seems to think needs a wall built for border control.

> Brad: "John, you've been out here for two hours with your binoculars and rifle and haven't hunted a single one. I'm telling you, you're not gonna get any this year."

> John: "I'm not letting this hunting license expire this year without tagging one. Besides, I think I found a bait it likes."

> Brad: *Squints* "One small barrel of pure maple syrup?"

> John: "Correction—one small *leaking* barrel of pure maple syrup."

> Brad: "You think it's gonna smell that and crawl out of its hiding place for *this*?"

> John: "A Canadian citizen looking to illegally cross the border into the United States won't ever ignore a poor, leaking, orphaned barrel of maple syrup. The native will want to secure it and bring it back home to its mother."

> Brad: *Grunts* "Right now, *I* want to go back home to *my* mother. She's making homemade apple crisp. And these mosquitos are driving me crazy!"

John: "Quitter!"

Brad: "Idiot!"

"The Spam Museum"

< Austin, Minnesota>

Its parent company Hormel has its home in Austin, Minnesota. Right next to the headquarters, you will find the mecca dedicated to the most famous preserved food sold under a brand name: Spam.

Rather than a misguided notion that the company is using it as a front to brainwash unsuspecting lost boys into being employed on the production line, the museum is a charming look at our nation's history during the World War eras when food was scarce and the means to afford it even more so.

Regardless of the modern cults who adore it and the critics who shun it, no one can take away the food's impact when Americans needed it the most.

Pat: "Don't make her eat it, Debra!"

Debra: "Pat, knock it off! It's really good, Maria. I grew up on this. You just have to try it first."

Maria: "I thought you said you eat it, Pat?!"

Pat: "Oh, I *eat* anything she makes. Doesn't mean I *like* it."

Debra: "That's it. Come on. Down the hatch, Maria!"

Maria: *Takes a bite*

<u>Debra</u>: "Well…?"

<u>Maria</u>: "I've made my decision. When it comes to Spam, I think…"

"Treasure Island Resort & Casino"

<Welch, Minnesota>

Hidden in the hills of Red Wing, the Prairie Island Indian Community runs the resort which reminds you every winter that in this world there is a tropical paradise with coconuts, palm trees, wild birds, and temperatures above 80 degrees every single day… and it's not here.

<u>Hank</u>: "Alice, I thought you said we were going to your sister's?"

<u>Alice</u>: "I told you: she got a room here tonight!"

<u>Hank</u>: "We've 'looked' at three slot machines now and haven't seen her yet."

<u>Alice</u>: "I'll just investigate this machine here, and then I'll give her a call."

<u>Hank</u>: "What do you mean 'investigate'? Did you forget your sister's phone number didn't start with '7-7-7' for an area code?!"

"World's Largest Ball of Twine"

\<Darwin, Minnesota>*

*created by a single person 1979-1994

Francis Johnson of Darwin created the phenomenon. It is 13 feet in diameter, 40 feet in circumference, and weighs 17,400 pounds. Why did he do it? Because we as a human race don't know what we need in life until we see it.

Linda: "This is the largest ball of twine?"

Randy: "Yup."

Linda: "Is there a ... video we're supposed to watch?"

Randy: "Nope."

Linda: "Is there a presentation we can sit through?"

Randy: "Nope."

Linda: "I see. ... ...What's that over there?"

Randy: "It's a tiny plaque and a donation box."

Linda: "Oh, I'm sure there's nothing in the donation box."

Randy: "Actually, there is! Oh, wait. No. That's just a sticky note."

Linda: "What does it say?"

Randy: "I owe you $5."

"Minnesota Educational Computing Consortium"

<Headquarters @ I don't know... the Capitol, I guess?>

Known as MECC, for short, this endeavor originated from the Minnesota State Legislature in 1971. The company was designed to promote the technology education that is responsible for many games which are still remembered by students who grew up in the 1980s and 1990s, including *The Secret Island of Dr. Quandary, Number Munchers, Word Munchers, Lemonade Stand,* and *DinoPark Tycoon.*

But the grand icon of them all was MECC's re-imagining of the 1971 text-only classic: *The Oregon Trail* created by Don Rawitsch, Bill Heinemann, and Paul Dillenberger. In 1985, MECC transformed it into the well-known visual experience which would later inspire other companies to continue its relevance even in 2022 with modern versions available on the Nintendo Switch, PC, and the internet-based software program Steam. How long has it been since *you* last died of dysentery?

> Charlie: "What a classic! Did you ever play that game growing up?"
>
> Jane: "Oh, yes. Couldn't get enough of it in elementary school."
>
> Jane's mother: "What was the point of that game again?"
>
> Charlie: "Get the settlers to the West before everyone in your party dies."

<u>Jane's mother</u>: "What a macabre game for little kids to play!"

<u>Charlie</u>: "No kidding. Especially since every time I played, the mother-in-law always died first from Scarlet Fever."

BOOK BREAK!

Before we say goodbye—the *real* meaning of the phrase "That's Different":

That's different.
   – I state: these two things are not alike.

THAT'S different.
   – I am very uncomfortable right now and would like to
   know the location of the nearest exit.

That's DIFFERENT.
   – I am surprised by this outcome, and I'm starting to
warm up to it.

That's ... different?
   – I am confused and can't express myself in any other way.

THAT'S DIFFERENT!
   – I say: let us celebrate the unique qualities!

FAMOUS PEOPLE

The term "famous" these days comes with a lot of connotations and really challenges the qualifications of such moniker. According to my mother, I was famous at 16 the minute I was put into the local newspaper in the district court records for a speeding violation. I am, however, happy to tell you, the standard for this is much higher as we go deeper into the state's history for stars, artists, and historical figures who have made a much bigger impression than just one viral sensation with a Tik-Tok video.

Famous People. And people who need famous people. Who needs them? Minnesotans do. We love our celebrities as ourselves and form a community around them that breaks borders, destroys boundaries, and crushes barriers. In other words: next time, use condoms.

And speaking of unused birth control, our next chapter will be told through the eyes of children. Why children? You won't find more honesty than through the eyes of heathens—I mean, children. Unfortunately, my inspiration on this was a bit dry as I haven't lived in the state for several years. Thus, I have forgotten the wealth of knowledge a child from Minnesota can bring.

To overcome that obstacle, I reached out to my friend Laura on social media and asked, and I quote, "Could I use your children to publicly exploit the state of Minnesota?" I have since reflected that perhaps I could have worded it differently as I am no longer allowed to contact my friend per the Olmsted County Sheriff. The silver lining to this mishap is I can certainly tell you, while on the phone, the police department there was, indeed, very nice.

In the end, I was able to find two spritely volunteers who one day may be Minnesota celebrities themselves. Let's see if you can figure out what they might be famous for one day...

Erica & Timothy Bennett
Mankato, Minnesota

Meet the Bennetts! They are a lovely family with the picturesque two-story home, torn-up sidewalk, a sinkhole in the yard from the spring thaw, a rusted chain-link fence, and a vicious guard dog ... named "Muffy." I went to school with *both* Mr. Bennett and Mrs. Bennett growing up and have come to the conclusion that neither of them knew how to date outside the school's feeder system.

After reflecting on my own hometown in which I had way too many "distant" cousins than logically possible in a small radius for someone *not* to be inbred, I bit my tongue and decided there were worse things than my former classmates "studying" underneath the bleachers between class periods back in the day. Thus, them having children was inevitable.

Erica is 11 years old and stepping her toes into the chaotic and ever-changing world of middle school. By her overall demeanor and disposition, she appears to be taking it in stride. She made the "A" Honor Roll all three quarters thus far and has high hopes for volleyball and track-and-field next year. The young girl looks exactly like her mother. Speaking optimistically, if the education system fails her, her looks will set her up for success.

Timothy is 9 years old. Enough said.

This is the segment—and *the* only segment—where I sat with both the Minnesota-grown residents to gather information and commentary on such a topic. I also need to be up front and honest by saying that I did provide Mr. and Mrs. Bennett with the list of celebrities and references beforehand so that I could have quality discussions. Here's what happened...

The Introduction

Erica, Timothy, and I were seated comfortably in the living room with our refreshments. (Before you ask, yes, I was offered coffee. But I had already brought my own from Starbucks. And it was a good thing too. I saw those instant coffee crystals sitting on the counter!) Mrs. Bennett sat at the adjacent kitchen table with her head propped up by her fully manicured hand—amused by it all. Mr. Bennett stood at the kitchen island, pretending to read the local newspaper. Erica sat there smiling, occasionally giggling to herself, unsure of what to expect. Timothy, God bless him, sat there annoyed and occasionally looked at the blank TV screen as if the interview had been scheduled during his favorite show. Throughout the beginning, Mr. Bennett constantly reminded his son to uncross his arms and sit up straight—neither trait he himself could do in the roughly 12 years I knew him.

> Lucas: "I'll introduce myself. I'm Lucas LaMont, and I'm writing a book about the many different topics of Minnesota. My stories are told through people having discussions, so I decided to try this next segment with kids from Minnesota. Your mom and dad said you two were really excited about doing this, so let's give it a shot, shall we?"

Erica: "Okay!"

Lucas: "Timothy?"

Timothy: *Nods*

Lucas: *Cautiously* "Let's start with a warm-up question before we get to discussing the famous people. What comes to mind when you think about Minnesota?"

Erica: "Snow. Lots and lots of snow."

Lucas: "And you, Tim?"

Timothy: "Football!"

Lucas: "You like football, huh? Who is your favorite sports team?"

Timothy: "Green Bay Packers!"

Lucas: *Bites lower lip* "I'm sure my readers are loving that."

Timothy: "TIMMY!"

Lucas: "I'm sorry?"

Erica: "He wants you to call him 'Timmy'!"

Lucas: "Like from *South Park*?"

Timothy: *Nods excitedly*

Lucas: "Your dad lets you watch *South Park*? You're nine."

Timothy: "Your dad let you write a book about Minnesota?"

Lucas: "He regrets a few things. And now, so do I." ***Clears throat***

At this point, Mr. and Mrs. Bennett tried to step in and intervene in their cherub's behavior—but I insisted I needed a completely unabashed and uninhibited approach to the interview to get my much-needed Minnesota moments.

Lucas: "Anyway, it doesn't matter. I can't call you 'TIMMY!' because I can't use your real names. When I rewrite this, I'm going to have to change the story and reference a different character. Otherwise, based upon the character, readers might be able to identify who you really are."

Erica: "Why is that bad?"

Lucas: "Not everyone in the world is a good person. It's a way of protecting yourself and who you are. Speaking of, that works well with the topic. Celebrities use alternative names when they become famous to help protect themselves too. With that, let's start with our first one..."

Defining a "Celebrity"

Lucas: "Let's start with Little Crow..."

Timothy: "I told my dad that some people on your list weren't celebrities."

Lucas: "Why so?"

Erica: "Because celebrities are like movie stars or singers."

Timothy: "Yeah. He's not on YouTube."

Lucas: "The word celebrity itself simply means 'well known.' And think about it, in the 1860s, did we have internet? Movies? TV?"

Erica/Timothy: "No."

Lucas: "So what do you think made people celebrities back then?"

Erica: "Important things they've done?"

Lucas: "Exactly! And what if I told you Little Crow and the Dakota people are, in fact, YouTube famous?"

Timothy: "Really?"

Lucas: "Uh-huh." ***Grabs phone and plays a YouTube video*** "See?"

Timothy: ***Squints*** "Little Crow cleaned kitchens?"

Lucas: "What?" ***Looks at phone*** "Oh, sorry. That's an ad for Mrs. Meyer's [Cleaning Products]. Here..."

Little Crow III (Little Crow)

[c. 1810 – July 3, 1863]
Native American Dakota Chief

Since Little Crow was one of the most prolific and influential Native Americans in the state, elementary and middle school classrooms will focus on the Dakota leader as the leader of the Sioux Uprising and Dakota War of 1862 which lasted five weeks. However, the Sioux also have an even bigger impact in the state by becoming experts in living/surviving on the plains while also playing a significant role in trading with the French in the Great Lakes Fur Trade.

Timothy: **After watching the YouTube video**
"He *is* famous!"

Lucas: "Erica—I asked your mom, and she said you had a Minnesota History class." **Points to her school textbook sitting on the table** "Did you learn about Little Crow?"

Erica: ***Nods***

Lucas: "What did you learn?"

Erica: "Little Crow was the leader of the Dakota tribe when there was a big war. The Dakota people were starving and struggling. It's also when the United States kept asking for more land to be given to the government."

Lucas: "Someone studied for this." ***Smirks***

A Moment for the State Flag

Lucas: "Timmy—do you know anything about Native Americans in Minnesota?"

Timothy: "They wore feathers."

Lucas: "I bet you know more than that." ***Whispers*** "Take a look at your sister's textbook."

Timothy: ***Looks*** "They're on the state flag!"

Lucas: "There you go!"

Erica: "My parents said they're going to change it soon."

Lucas: "Sounds like it. What do you think about that?"

Erica: "I like the flag. I don't want them to change it."

Timothy: "Me neither."

Lucas: "Do you know why some want to change the flag to begin with?"

Erica: "People say it's racist."

Timothy: "What does that word mean?"

Lucas: "Racist means you judge people by their skin color. You assume people act in a certain way, talk in a certain way, or have a certain level of intelligence based upon it."

Erica: "How is the flag racist if Indians at that time looked like that?"

Lucas: "Maybe it's more than that. If you look at the flag, we have a European settler working on the land while a Native American is riding by on a horse. Let's go back to what you said about Little Crow and the Dakota tribes. The United States Government wanted more land from them, right?"

Erica: "Yeah."

Lucas: "Do you think Native Americans would have minded sharing the land they wanted?"

Timothy: "No."

Lucas: "No, I don't think so either. But is that what happened when Native Americans signed those treaties? Were they sharing it anymore?"

Erica: "No. Native Americans had to stay on their own land."

Lucas: "Right. In a treaty, you sign a deal. And that was the deal. But you said it yourself, Erica: Native Americans were struggling at the time. And do you think Natives before European settlers came along ever imagined they'd one day have people come onto their land and say one day 'We own this now. You keep out'?"

Erica: ***Shakes head***

Lucas: "What emotions do you think some Native Americans have when they look at our state flag?"

Erica: "It reminds them of what they don't have anymore."

Timothy: "But they do have land. They live on reservations."

Lucas: "Minnesota has about 51 million acres of land in the state.* Native Americans own 56 million acres throughout the entire country.** That's near the land size of the entire state. We have 50 states in our country. Split Minnesota into 50 pieces. Do you think that's a lot of land for Native Americans who once thought the land across the entire country was free for everyone to use?"

Erica: "No."

Lucas: "Think that might contribute to how they feel about our flag?"

Erica: "Yeah."

Lucas: "I think so too."

* According to Minnesota Department of Natural Resources

** According to the United States of the Interior

Alexander Ramsey

[September 8, 1815–April 22, 1903]
First Minnesota Territorial Governor

This politician is equally synonymous with Minnesota, like Little Crow. Ramsey is noted for solidifying governmental control of the state and the defenses for the Sioux Uprising and Dakota War of 1862. He represented the Whig and Republican political parties, and from 1879 to 1881, he even served as the Secretary of War under President Rutherford Hayes.

Lucas: "Let's move on. Next, we have Alexander Ramsey, one of two Minnesota politicians we're going to talk about today. He represents the United States' response at the time to expand government control over new territories and states. [He's] also credited with helping make Minnesota what it is today and even was the first governor of the territory."

Timothy: "What makes him so special?"

Lucas: "He's actually a last-minute addition I made once I knew I was coming here. Can you think of a reason why?" **No response** "Think about the street you live on."

Erica: "Ramsey Street!"

Lucas: "And guess who it's named after?"

Timothy: "Alexander Ramsey?"

Lucas: "You got it. Did you know you lived on a street named after a celebrity?"

Erica: "I want a street with my name on it."

Lucas: "Erica Drive? Erica Avenue?"

Erica: "Ooo, I like that one!"

Lucas: "How about Lucas Lane?"

Timothy: "TIMMY! Street!"

Lucas: "That too."

Sinclair Lewis (Harry Sinclair Lewis)

[February 7, 1885–January 10, 1951]
1930 Nobel Prize Winner in Literature

Sinclair Lewis was a novelist experiencing massive critical and commercial success in the 1910s and 1920s with notable titles such as *Main Street* [1920], *Babbitt* [1922], and *Arrowsmith* [1925]. In 1930, he was awarded the Nobel Prize for creating well-developed characters while shining a spotlight on everything America wasn't versus everything it was.

Erica: "What does 'exploit' mean?"

Lucas: "It means you hyperfocus on one idea so that's all people will give attention to or think about. Unfortunately, it's mostly used in a negative way or only used on whatever gets people superficial success."

Erica: "Why would he get a prize for that?"

Lucas: "Sinclair did what you call 'satire.'"

Timothy: "What's that?"

Lucas: "That's when you focus on the unusual, unique, strange, or sometimes even wrong concepts people believe and do and make it appear like that's what everyone does. Most of the time, it's done out of humor. Sinclair Lewis did that a lot with his books. He focused on people who lived in the Midwest and even Minnesota and portrayed it like people here were small-minded, simple, or even backward in their thinking."

Erica: "Who actually thinks it's a good idea to write a book where you make fun of people in Minnesota?"

Lucas: *Gulps and swallows existential crisis* "No one I know."

Judy Garland (Frances Ethel Gumm)

[June 10, 1922– June 22, 1969]
Actress and Singer

She was born a small-town girl from Grand Rapids, but today Judy Garland is the most iconic actress to come from our amazing state—and we all know why. L. Frank Baum wrote *The Wonderful Wizard of Oz* in 1900, and in 1939, *The Wizard of Oz* film cemented itself as the quint-essential American fairy tale. Garland's performance was elevated further by her rendition of "Somewhere Over the Rainbow," which was named Recording Industry Association of America (RIAA) / National Endowment for the Arts' (NEA) #1 Song of the Century and American Film Institute's (AFI) #1 Song in a film.

Lucas: "Since you both have seen the movie, why don't you tell me your favorite part."

Erica: "When she melts the witch in the end!"

Timothy: "I like the flying monkeys."

Erica: ***Turns to her brother*** "Not in the movie. In the *cartoon*—they are funny. In the movie—they're creepy!"

Timothy: "No, they're cool!"

Lucas: "I grew up with the movie and I have to agree with Timmy." ***Shocking, I know*** "The flying monkeys were cool."

Erica: "Was that your favorite part?"

Lucas: "My favorite part was in the beginning when the twister hit. But I'm partial to severe storms."

Erica: "What happened to [Judy Garland] after *The Wizard of Oz*?"

Lucas: "She went on to have a very successful movie career and an extraordinary singing career as well. She is also the mother of Liza Minnelli, who followed in her mother's foot-steps. Unfortunately, Judy was also a great example of how fame can be dangerous if it becomes overwhelming and unregulated. She died when she was only 47."

Erica: "She went over the rainbow and back to Oz."

Lucas: *Smiles* "Maybe she did. Maybe she did."

Winona Ryder (Winona Laura Horowitz)

[October 29, 1971-]
Actress

Any connoisseur of 1980s and 1990s nostalgia will recall several notable films Winona Ryder starred in: *Beetlejuice* [1988], *Heathers* [1989], *Edward Scissorhands* [1990], and *Girl, Interrupted* [1999]. But even Winona Ryder couldn't have predicted the overwhelming success the series *Stranger Things* would become. Ryder has received critical acclaim and several award nominations for her portrayal of the character Joyce Byers. I'm told her character never shoplifted once! (Guess they weren't type-casting.)

Lucas: "I sent your parents a very long list of both actors and actresses from Minnesota and lo and behold, a show about the Demogorgon is what I heard it took for you two to recognize someone."

Erica: "I love that show! Love that song!"

Lucas: "Which one?"

Erica: "'Running Up That Hill.'"

Lucas: "Ah, yes. Kate Bush." ***Looks at Timothy*** "Doesn't the show scare you at all?"

Timothy: "No way! In fact, I wanted to be a Demogorgon for Halloween."

Lucas: "You wouldn't have even needed a costume."

Timothy: "Huh?"

Lucas: "Nothing." ***Switches topics*** "Winona Ryder is said to be named after the city Winona, Minnesota, which means she's doubly representing our state. She and the original cast have come back for *Beetlejuice 2*."

Erica: "Mom and I watched the first one. We can't wait."

Timothy: ***Stares at me*** "What did you mean when you said I wouldn't need a costume to be a Demogorgon?"

Lucas: "Moving on!"

Bob Dylan (Robert Allen Zimmerman)

[May 24, 1941-]
Singer/songwriter

Bob Dylan's lyrics and music struck a chord with the nation during the 1960s when the world was on fire from political movements against inequality, war, and the lack of government transparency. Several famous songs include "Blowin' in the Wind" [1963] and "The Times They Are a-Changin'" [1964]. 40 albums later, he's an American staple and Minnesota treasure.

Lucas: *Looks at Mr. and Mrs. Bennett* "Alright, Mom and Dad, this one is for you."

Mr. Bennett: "My dad used to listen to his albums on vinyl when I was a kid."

Mrs. Bennett: "My parents had them, too. How about yours?"

Lucas: "I think my mom had an album of his. But I found out about Bob Dylan just like any 90s kid found out about Bob Dylan—that one scene from *Forrest Gump* when Jennie sings in the … um … 'variety show.'"

Mr. Bennett: "Good movie. Good scene." *Mrs. Bennett looks back* "What?"

Lucas: "As bad as it is to say, it wasn't until the movie *The Watchmen* [2009] when I heard 'The Times They Are a-Changin'.' What I can say from that is Bob Dylan has crossed into the mainstream over 50 years later and is still relevant today. How many artists can say that?"

John Earl Madden

[April 10, 1936 – December 28, 2021]
Head Coach of the Oakland Raiders [1969-1978] & National Football League (NFL) Sports Commentator.

If Spam alone wasn't enough to put Austin, Minnesota, into epic territory, then perhaps the legendary John Madden will do it. Madden led the Oakland Raiders to several great seasons in the NFL, including Superbowl Champions in 1976. In 1988, he headlined one of the most successful sports video game series ever under *John Madden Football* and later *Madden NFL.*

Lucas: "'Are you ready for some football?'"

Mr. Bennett: "I even played those games as a kid."

Timothy: "That game rules."

Lucas: "Timmy, which one did you play last?"

Timothy: "My friend has *Madden 22* on PS4. We play that."

Lucas: "Do I dare ask what team you play as?"

Timothy: "[Green Bay] Packers!"

Lucas: "... ... ... do you want to just lie and say 'Minnesota Vikings' instead?"

Timothy: "No. Why?"

Lucas: "So my readers don't think I sold out to 'the enemy.'"

Timothy: "What do I get out of it?"

Lucas: "A signed copy of the book I'm writing when it comes out?"

Timothy: "Nah."

Lucas: "I can't believe it; I'm losing my ego to a 9-year-old Packers fan." ***Sighs*** "There are several icons in the NFL, but only one name has consistently graced every single edition of a sponsored video game—and that is John Madden himself. If that isn't a legacy, I don't know what is." ***Looks at Timothy*** "You have the late John Madden to thank for all those games—even if you do choose the Green Bay Packers."

Erica: "I like the Minnesota Vikings!"

Lucas: "There is a God."

Jesse Ventura (James George Janos)

[July 15, 1951]
Former professional wrestler and politician
Governor of Minnesota [1999-2003]

Minneapolis-born James George Janos probably wasn't in school drawing up Venn-Diagrams on the comparisons and contrasts of being a professional wrestler and government politician, but if he was—I bet they were fascinating. How an oiled-up bodybuilding wrestler screaming insults in a tight speedo and feather boa successfully dons a business suit and becomes the voted face of decorum for an entire state, I'll never know. But stranger things have happened!

> Lucas: *Searches for a picture of on my phone* "Erica, Timothy, I give you the wildcard of Minnesota. Our former state governor: Jesse 'The Body' Ventura."

> Erica: *Mouth open wide* "What is he wearing?"

> Mrs. Bennett: *Looks over* "More like, what isn't he wearing?"

> Lucas: "Believe it or not, Jesse Ventura had a career to wear that as his uniform. He was well-known in the 1970s and 1980s for being a loud, flamboyant personality until he retired due to health reasons."

> Timothy: "Well, what he did he do after that?"

> Lucas: "What every retired professional wrestler does—run for political office."

> Timothy. "Oh."

Erica: "Did he act like that when he was governor?"

Lucas: "No, he was much more mainstream like you would expect anyone else at their job. But he was known for giving his honest opinion, and that did rub a few people the wrong way. As far as his venture in office and what he's known for..." ***Looks at Mr. Bennett***

Mr. Bennett: "Fireworks?"

Lucas: "That's true: Minnesota did legalize fireworks during his time in office."

Erica: "Awesome!"

Timothy: "Cool! A wrestler and a guy who gives us fireworks? He's my favorite from Minnesota!"

Lucas: "Don't you want to hear how he represented a completely different political party and shook up 'politics as usual' and still became successful despite all the opposition he faced?"

Timothy: "Did he body slam anyone when he was in office?"

Lucas: "No."

Timothy: "Then, no."

Charles Monroe Schulz

[November 26, 1922–February 12, 2000]
Cartoonist most known for comic strip *Peanuts*

What would the world be like without Charlie Brown and his dog Snoopy? Luckily, we don't have to know. In addition to his famous comic strip, which ran from 1950-2000, many fans still enjoy the famous holiday TV specials, the *Peanuts Movie* [2015], and even the musical!

Lucas: "Now here is one I am personally excited to discuss."

Erica: "Snoopy!"

Timothy: "Charlie Brown!" ***Immediately hops up*** "I can do the Charlie Brown dance." ***Shows off his mad skills***

Lucas: "Impressive. But can you do the Macarena?"

Timothy: "The what?"

Lucas: "Never mind."

Erica: "We watch the Thanksgiving and Christmas Special in school every year."

Timothy: "Yeah. They set it up in the gym on the big screen."

Lucas: "What do you think makes the *Peanuts* gang so popular? The series is almost 75 years old, yet kids today know exactly what it is. I can't say that about the Macarena."

Timothy: "What's the Macarena?"

Lucas: "It was a 90s thing. Dark period in our history. It was one of the only things the world could agree on at the time."

Erica: "Everyone knows all the characters: Lucy, Linus, Woodstock, Schroder and his piano."

Lucas: "He really did develop characters, which were unique. And you need to remember, a comic strip was only about 3-5 pictures which told a short message or story. But [Schultz] always had a message that related to his audience. In fact, if you read his very first comic, Schultz exercises a very 'Minnesota Nice' trait."

Timothy: "Which one?"

Lucas: ***Pulls out phone and locates issue #1*** "You tell me."

Timothy: "The boy says he likes Charlie Brown to his face but then says he 'hates him' to the girl after he leaves. That's 'Minnesota Nice'?"

Lucas: "Very much so."

Timothy: "How so?"

Lucas: "If I was to ask you right now if you enjoyed this interview, what would you say?"

Timothy: "I liked it."

Lucas: "After I leave, what are you going to tell Mom and Dad?"

Timothy: "... ... ..."

Lucas: "Timmy, you are a pure Minnesotan already."

And there you have it, folks! I hope at the end of this book, you are now more confident than ever on your ability to meld into Minnesota culture. If you aren't, I was told by a friend this book made a lot more sense after her third glass of wine—whatever that means. She was also disappointed I didn't talk about the "Paul Bunyan and Babe the Blue Ox" statues located in Bemidji or the wonder that is the "beef commercial sandwich." To both comments, I say this: Minnesota is what you make it. And if you find it your local church cookbook, you'll make it even better. Now *that's* Minnesota Nice!

Want more information on the topics presented here?
Please utilize the sources listed here:

Anoka Halloween	anokahalloween.com	"The History of Anoka Halloween Capital of the World"
Associated Press	bigstory.ap.org	"Oshie latest success story from tiny Minn. town"
Business Journal: Minneapolis/St. Paul	bizjournals.com	"Caribou founder: Knowing when to leave the corporate world and go into business for yourself"
CBSNews: Minnesota	cbsnews.com	"The story behind Faribault County's Jolly Green Giant statue"
Chanhassen Dinner Theatres	chanhassendt.com	"About Chanhassen Dinner Theatres"
Duluth Stories	duluthstories.net	"Contact & Fur Trade"
Experience Rochester, Minnesota	experiencerochestermn.com	"The Ear of Corn Water Tower: The History of Rochester's Beloved Landmark"
Food Dive	fooddive.com	"Hormel Foods' snack brands thrive behind 'transformative' $3.35B Planters buy"
Frank Lloyd Wright	franklloydwright.org	"Lindholm Oil Company Service Station"
General Mills	generalmills.com	"Our History"
Historical Marker Database	hmdb.org	"A Golden Dedication for I-90"
Historically Speaking	vugradhistory.wordpress.com	Where Did The Land O'Lakes Logo Come From?
Hormel	www.hormelfoods.com	"Our History"

Organization	URL	Title
Mayo Clinic	history.mayoclinic.org	"Mayo Clinic History and Heritage"
Minnesota Educational Computing Consortium	Mecc.co	"Home"
New York Times	https://www.nytimes.com	"Spam Turns Serious and Hormel Turns Out More"
Pillsbury	pillsbury.com	"How Well Do You Know the Pillsbury Doughboy?"
Roadside America	roadsideamerica.com	"Biggest Ball of Twine in Minnesota"
Spam Museum	spam.com	"What is Spam Brand?"
Star Tribune	startribune.com	"Best Buy, by the years"
TripSavvy	tripsavvy.com	"The Best Juicy Lucy Burger in Minneapolis"
Visit Warroad	visitwarroad.com	"History of Warroad"

(There are no coupons for any Hormel
products at the end of this book.)

AUTHOR BIO

Lucas LaMont lives near the mountains of Colorado and has been a storyteller since childhood. Throughout the years, he has dabbled in fiction and poetry, and in his adult writing, most of his focus has been in gay fiction. Recently, he discovered the Omegaverse genre and is obsessed with it! During the Covid pandemic, he found his favorite series to read: The Adrien English Mysteries by Josh Lanyon (But he is very much a fan of several noteworthy Omegaverse authors). When he's not writing and reading, Lucas loves traveling to fabulous Las Vegas to gamble or staying near the rustic lakes of Minnesota to go fishing. The goal of his writing has always been to focus on the power of relationships and the journey they take. You can find Lucas Lamont on Facebook, Twitter, Instagram, and Wix.

Discover more at
4HorsemenPublications.com

10% off using HORSEMEN10

Milton Keynes UK
Ingram Content Group UK Ltd.
UKHW042145281024
450365UK00010B/629

9 798823 204293